Loss and learning disability

Noelle
Blackman

D1390709

Worth Publishing

www.worthpublishing.com

First published 2003 by Worth Publishing Ltd
6 Lauderdale Parade, London W9 1LU
www.worthpublishing.com

Printed and bound in Great Britain by Bath Press, Bath, UK

British Library Cataloguing in Publication Data
A catalogue record for this book is available from the British Library

ISBN 1-9032690-24

Table 5.2 from *Loss and Bereavement* by Sheila Payne (1999) (Open University Press) reproduced on p. 16 with kind permission of Open University Press and Professor Sheila Payne.
The account of Jane on p. 61 is drawn from the writing of Maureen Oswin (1989), with kind permission of the King's Fund, London
Letter reproduced on pp. 125-126 with kind permission of *Community Living*

Front cover photograph and design by John Stanyon
Text design by Caroline Harper

Acknowledgements

My greatest thanks of all go to the bereaved people with learning disabilities who I have had the privilege to support. I have learned so much from each of them. My next thanks go to Irma Mullins, my line manager at roc, for her commitment to the Loss and Bereavement service and for her great support of me in this work. Without her energy and enthusiasm, the service could never have been established. I would like to thank all the clinical supervisors (too many to name) that I have had over the years; the very first one being Andrea (Perry) Wood, who went on to encourage me to write this book and who has been infinitely patient and supportive in her more recent role as editor and publisher. Other supervisors include Katharine Collingwood, my dear friend and colleague; and finally the person who has taught me so much and who has helped me to find confidence in my own practice through her tireless encouragement, Valerie Sinason.

I would also like to extend my thanks to colleagues, past and present, from the team at roc - Tracey-Jo Simpson, Caroline Owen, Sarah Robertson, Alison Butterfield, Lyn Huddleston and Peter Iweanya. In particular I would like to acknowledge my good friend and colleague at roc, David O'Driscoll, for all that I have learned through thinking, talking and working with him. Thanks to Avril and Gill at Harperbury library for their tremendous help.

Thanks to David Thompson for all that I have gained from working alongside him, and for all the opportunities that he has offered me. And to Linda McEnhill for all that she has taught me about palliative care, for her support and for her friendship. For the idea for the cover and the beautiful photograph I would like to thank John Stanyon. A huge thank you to my Mum and Chris for all that they have done to help me finally get this book written.

Finally, but by no means least, I want to give the greatest thanks to Peter, Harry and Florrie, for putting up with me during the writing of this book.

In memory of Maureen Oswin (1931-2001),
whose courageous research and writing
first inspired my work.

Contents

Preface

The Lord Rix CBE DL

Bereavement ranks alongside sex, voting and managing money as something from which we have tried to protect people with learning disabilities - rather than helping them to live through it as positively as possible. I can see why. It isn't just the old myth of perpetual childhood, and inability to cope with adult things; it is the reality that for all of us, bereavement is hard to handle. It doesn't become any easier when you reach my age and have, inevitably, experienced rather a lot of it.

The fundamental message from this book is that only those who have nobody to love never experience the loss of someone they care about.... and, as Tennyson noted, never having anyone to care about is an even worse loss than losing someone you have cared about.

> I hold it true, whate'er befall:
> I feel it, when I sorrow most;
> 'Tis better to have loved and lost
> Than never to have loved at all.
> (*"In Memoriam"*)

Since people with learning disabilities cannot be protected against loss, it is no kindness to deny them the opportunity to grieve in their own way and at their own pace; and here in the pages that follow are suggestions as to how that can be supported. There is good practice to copy, and there is an evidence base to build on, although still a slender one. Noelle Blackman shares what she and others have found to work.

Things have moved on, and we are less inclined than once we were to duck telling people that someone they loved is dead – on the bland assumption that they will find an apparently intentional absence less upsetting than the enforced absence of death. However, it does us no harm at all to be reminded of just how much loss and smothered grief our (usually well-intentioned) social policies have inflicted on people with learning disabilities. Some people entered hospitals with their parents and siblings alive, and thereafter had little contact with them alive, and no information about their deaths. Others lived with an elderly parent until that parent died, and were then whipped away to an unfamiliar place with people they didn't know, having no stake in the funeral. There they depended for consolation on people who knew nothing of their family, had no baseline of knowing the non-grieving individual, and who lacked personal experience of bereavement.

There is of course always the danger of jumping from ignoring grief to clinicalising it. Hence the need to hang on to the recognition that handling the loss of someone you love is a very personal thing. Given the rich diversity of ways those without disabilities handle loss, we should be very cautious about treating any reaction by someone with a learning disability as morbid. Particularly where someone is not able to read about death and mourning, struggles with concepts of death (and resurrection), and is unable to put their feelings into words, living through a death and its after-math is bound to be idiosyncratic. Patient companionship is not a bad response. Always assume that a person with a learning disability who has been bereaved is more aware than you are inclined to think they are. Don't undervalue the importance of tangible tokens of the lost relation-ship. Don't assume that people who say nothing have forgotten.

For so long, we got it wrong. Maybe now we can get it right.

The Lord Rix CBE DL
London

Foreword

Valerie Sinason

When there are issues in our lives which we cannot bear and wish to disown, we often call them "Life Events". The term carries with it the wish that we could incorporate such subjects into our lives and take them for granted. We cannot. Indeed, as often happens, the term becomes a euphemism, a verbal way of covering up the painful rawness of the topic.

Death is the ultimate event we cannot bear, and is therefore subject to a large number of euphemisms. The brilliant British writer and actor, John Cleese, provided the ultimate example of this with an episode concerning a dead parrot in the "Monty Python" television series. The parrot, clearly dead and nailed to its perch, was called all the euphemisms under the sun in the attempt to let its besotted owner realise the bird was dead. The loud catalogue of euphemistic terms - a "gone parrot", a "passed-away parrot" were comically defused. Humour attempts to deal with the pain of our mortality by bringing it to the conscious surface in a form that is tolerable. "You want to know if you are dying, Mrs. Smith?" asked the GP. "Madam, that will be the last thing you do".

Death is the open secret we carry. Although it applies to all of us, we have rarely been able to deal with it societally in the contemporary West. Widows and widowers, grieving parents, grieving children, grieving friends, often find themselves left alone after the initial outpouring of compassionate feelings. Even the new understanding of the stages of bereavement is used as a dissociative defence against the pain of personal loss or another's loss: "Oh well, that's normal for mourning, and it will take you a year to stop feeling mad".

What then happens when we link the universal taboo of death with the taboo subject of learning disability? Our society, which so privileges mental cognitive ability, is only just beginning to value its citizens with a learning disability. Having a mind that cannot perform at the same level as others of the same chronological age evokes guilt and fear. We disown our learning disabled citizens by either placing them out of the reach of the rest of society, or by bringing them into an area we choose to call "community" without adequately enabling empowerment and inclusion.

People with learning disabilities have to face death in themselves, and particularly, in their parents. Sheila Hollins, Pat Frankish and I have all written on the crucial theme of extra dependency needs in people with learning disabilities and the struggles to find a way of achieving psychic independence. Whilst developmental processes in young people usually leads, in the West, to psychic and physical separation from parents, this is often not possible for adolescents and young people with disabilities. Care in the community for a fifty year old man with a learning disability can be his eighty year old mother. Sometimes the lack of physical separation is enforced through lack of funding to allow more independent living; sometimes the parent her or himself has to maintain the caring role in the absence of a trusted service. Whilst there are some superb community homes and villages, there are still large areas without adequate resources.

A parent's death, as Noelle Blackman points out so beautifully, can bring a double trauma. The person with the disability often loses their home at the same time as losing a parent, and then has to face the physical upheaval of moving at the same time as mourning. They are all too often not included in the funeral arrangements. Disturbed behaviour, due to the bereavement process not being supported, distracts professionals all too often from the underlying pain.

This book is a timely, pioneering and profoundly moving aid in work with learning disabled people and fellow professionals. Noelle Blackman has the emotional capacity to focus on this painful double area of grief, both clinically and academically. She is at the forefront of bereavement studies as a teacher, lecturer, clinician and thinker. She can consider here the spiritual issues, the practical (for example, not even receiving a condolences card), the diagnostic issue of assessing grief response, the clinical and cultural. The client's voice is also poignantly represented. This book has been long-awaited from Noelle, and will provide a practical and emotional resource for all in the field.

Introduction

Over the last century, there has been a rise in the population of adults with learning disabilities in the UK. A major contributing factor to this rise has been an increase in life expectancy, due to the benefits of improved medical treatment, and to better living conditions. Both of these improvements have affected the longevity of the entire UK population. Whilst there are no definitive statistics for the number of people with learning disabilities living in the UK, it is recognised that there are more than 1.5 million people in the UK with learning disabilities, ranging from the mild/moderate, to severe and profound. The issues raised in this book, therefore, affect at least 3% of the UK population. If people with learning disabilities are living longer, they are more likely to experience at least one or more significant bereavements in their lifetime. This book addresses the fact that many of these people will not receive adequate consideration or sensitive treatment at this time. Research (Hollins & Esterhuyzen 1997) suggests that only 54% of people with learning disabilities attend their parents' funerals. The grief, suffering and loneliness of people with learning disabilities who have been bereaved still largely goes unnoticed, and may lead to behaviour which can cause further pain, difficulties and tensions not only for the individual concerned, but for families, workers, and the wider society around them.

Historically, people's emotional development has not been considered as separate to their intellectual development. The pioneering social researcher Maureen Oswin (1982) challenged the commonly held view that people with intellectual disabilities did not understand death and therefore could not grieve, instigating a slow change in society's thinking. The situation today has not moved very far forward, but there is some progress. There are promising, if rare, signs, such as when populist culture begins to take up the issue. I was very pleased, for example, to see the television drama series *Casualty* (BBC) include a story of a young bereaved woman with Down's syndrome in one of their Saturday night episodes.

But why is a change in thinking so slow to come about? And what can be done to improve the situation? Perhaps it is too difficult to acknowledge that people with learning disabilities have feelings. If we really allow ourselves to see the emotional pain that is so present for many people, due to trauma, to lack of control over their lives, to loss, to abuse, to social exclusion and to loneliness, then perhaps we would feel completely overwhelmed. It also seems sometimes that people with learning disabilities unconsciously recognise a need to protect the world and themselves from their own internal pain. This need becomes hidden behind 'the handicapped smile' to which Sinason (1992) so eloquently draws our attention. Perhaps this goes some way towards explaining why for so long the emotional and psychological needs of people with learning disabilities have been ignored. This book aims to contribute to the change in thinking which Oswin began.

My passion about the importance of this work began nearly fifteen years ago. I was working as a drama teacher in a further education college with people with learning disabilities.

One day, in a class for people who had severe learning disabilities, a student, who was always an anxious man, came into the room looking particularly distressed. I asked if anyone knew why he might be upset. I was told that he was in respite care because his father had been taken ill. The next week he seemed very withdrawn. I asked about his situation, and was told that he was still in respite care. In fact, his father had died several days previously, but no one was supposed to tell him. I was appalled; but even now, I am ashamed to admit that I colluded with everyone else, and neither told the man the news nor even found out who was going to tell him or what support, if any, he was getting. He stopped coming to my classes. I never knew the outcome to that man's story, although I could guess that it was not a very happy one. But I have often thought about him since.

Some time after this experience, I came across Maureen Oswin's seminal work *Am I allowed to cry?* (1991, Souvenir Press). Her book literally changed my life. I suddenly recognised the awful situations in which so many of the people I was working with were living. Many of my students were having to make sense of difficult and upsetting changes in their lives on their own; their grief was unacknowledged by everyone around them. I began to see things in a different light.

Simon, for example, was a man who attended a day centre where I worked once a week. Every time he saw me, he asked me how my father was (he asked everyone the same question). Reading Oswin's book prompted me to find out a little bit more about Simon's life. I discovered something that no-one had made any connections to before. His father had recently died; yet very few of the people who worked with Simon knew this information. I believe that Simon was repeatedly asking the same question because he was trying to make sense of his father's death. He needed to talk about it, and he wanted to find out if this happened to other people too. But no-one around him understood this; they just jollied him along, often not answering his question or not taking time to understand what he was really asking.

More and more, I began to recognise situations like this. At the same time as I was learning to appreciate the extent of pain in the lives of many of my students, I started a part-time training to become a dramatherapist. Once qualified, I began working for an organisation then known as Playtrac, a small service within a NHS Trust which provided training to direct care staff working with people with learning disabilities. This gave me the opportunity to write and run a training course on loss and bereavement, which proved to be very popular. But I discovered in running it that staff were concerned that when the people they were supporting experienced difficulty grieving, and needed more support than they felt that they could offer, they could not find any counselling or therapy services to which they could refer people with learning disabilities. This led to my proposal to set up what was to become the **roc** Loss and Bereavement service (Blackman 1999).

This is a service which offers therapy to people with learning disabilities, who experience difficulties connected to a bereavement or loss. It is the only service of its kind in the UK, to my knowledge. A vital component of the **roc** loss and bereavement intervention is the working partnership that is set up with the support system surrounding the individual, established through a two-day training programme. Many of the referrals are linked to behavioural problems; often disturbed behaviour may be seen as an expression of psychological needs not having been met. These are three examples of referrals made to **roc**:

- A man who was self-injuring after the death of a close female friend, with whom he had lived
- A man displaying bizarre behaviour after the death of his brother, including spending large lengths of time watching strangers' funerals
- A woman involved in 'searching' behaviour triggered by the loss of a close member of staff, but linked to the death of her mother

Times are changing, and with the introduction of the UK Government White Paper *Valuing People* (2001) there are moves to make services more integrated. In principle, I think this is a good thing. However, I am nervous that if integration happens too quickly, skills built up by workers in this field will get lost. At this moment in time, I believe that there is still a place for such a specialised learning disability bereavement service. I feel it is only through being specialised that we have grown in experience, and have had impact on local services through improving bereavement awareness. It is, of course, important to ensure that mainstream professionals acquire the knowledge of the specific needs and experiences of people with learning disabilities, and crucial, above all, that bereavement is better understood by everyone who may be in the role of supporting someone with a learning disability.

It is this need to share all that I have learned that has prompted me to write this book. It is aimed to be of use to families, direct care staff, learning disability professionals, generic professionals, counsellors and therapists. Many of the people I have worked with have given me permission to share their experiences with you, the reader, in the hope that this book will help other people going through their own bereavement. As well as case material, I draw on a broad foundation of past and current research and open up questions for further consideration.

The book begins with a chapter considering grief and mourning from a broad perspective. This first chapter explores the way in which the western world has attempted to understand these processes, and places the search for meaning within a historical context.

The second chapter reflects upon the critical gaze society places on people with learning disabilities, exploring in particular 'society's death wish' (Sinason 1992) and the effect that this may have on people with learning disabilities and their families in the context of coping with death and grief.

It concludes with a case history of the hospitalisation of a young man, which highlights many of the themes of this chapter.

The third chapter examines research on childhood bereavement. Understanding the way in which the knowledge of mortality is gained, and how we develop the capacity to cope with grief, may throw more light on some of the complex and varied factors which can affect the grieving process for someone with a learning disability. This chapter also considers attachment theory, and, from this perspective, considers the relationships between a disabled child and their parents particularly in light of the death of the parent. The chapter concludes by considering the environmental factors surrounding a person with a learning disability and reflecting on how these may hinder a healthy grieving process.

Chapter 4 highlights the prevalent disregard for the grief of people with learning disabilities. This chapter focuses on how grief may be expressed through behaviour. The 'grief' behaviour may not be understood as an expression of mourning and may lead the person into a cycle of behaviour which is labelled as challenging, which is, in turn, responded to punitively. The chapter culminates with some thoughts about how cycles of extreme behaviour triggered by grief can lead to some people with learning disabilities spending many years in and out of secure units, their grief still unacknowledged.

The fifth chapter examines some additional and often unrecognised losses that may occur when a parent dies. It is common, for example, for people with learning disabilities to move from the parental home into residential care immediately after the death of a parent. An experience of profound loss may reawaken painful feelings from other losses. This chapter examines other major losses that are common in the lives of people with a learning disability.

Chapter 6 considers the use of counselling and therapy. Historically, people with learning disabilities have not been considered suitable for any of the 'talking cures'. However, the climate has slowly begun to change recently, and many practitioners are finding that this client group can benefit fully from these types of intervention. Counselling or therapy is usually only necessary if there are complications in the grieving process. People with learning disabilities are highly likely to experience complications and are therefore more likely to be in need of support at this time. This chapter offers guidance to generic counsellors and therapists who are considering working with this client group. Chapter 7 continues with this guidance but also expands to consider how families and staff can also offer support.

The previous two chapters explored the use of therapy and counselling. Chapter 8 continues in the same vein by thinking specifically about the benefits and difficulties connected to running groups with people with learning disabilities. Groups encourage sharing of experience, listening to each other, learning and curiosity. The chapter examines two different models: bereavement therapy groups and death education groups.

Chapter 9 focuses on the stigma of disability, and how rejection and exclusion affects the lives of people with learning disabilities. Part of the chapter considers the effect this has on people as they become aware of their own mortality. It asks the question that was once asked of me by a client: "Will anyone care when I die?"

The final chapter, Chapter 10, offers ideas for training and developing good practice, focussed particularly on residential homes, but also including ideas for generic practitioners and for families.

Over the years, I have come across many people with learning disabilities who have experienced significant loss, in services for people with 'challenging behaviour', such as secure units, or, at the worst end of the spectrum, in forensic units. Often their grief has been unacknowledged. For example, I have come across individuals with learning disabilities locked up in forensic units for serious crimes, such as manslaughter and arson. On asking about these people's lives, I have been told that they have experienced bereavement, or other painful losses, and that they have had little, if any, support with this. Each of these people has difficulty in expressing themselves. Significantly, in each situation, the crimes committed seem to have happened around the anniversary of the person's significant loss. These examples suggest that more research is needed in order to establish definitive connections, but if bereavement and its effects were more widely understood, perhaps some situations of this kind could be prevented.

There are many moving real life stories within the pages of this book. But out in the world, there are even more people with learning disabilities whose loss goes by unnoticed, or whose expressions of grief are misunderstood. If this book can improve the quality of life for even one of these people, then I feel it will have achieved something worthwhile.

Chapter 1

Bereavement, mourning and grief

Bereavement is universal in humankind, and it has been argued that other sentient species share some aspects of and reactions to it.
(Payne et al 1999)

I thought I could describe a state; make a map of sorrow. Sorrow however turns out not to be a state but a process. It needs not a map but a history.
(Lewis 1961)

This chapter sets out to define our understanding of bereavement within a historical context, to provide a backdrop to the more complex area of bereavement and its meaning for people with learning disabilities. I shall examine theories and models of grief and mourning, which are based on clinical experience and empirical research, reflecting on the expected outcomes of the state of bereavement and how views on this have developed over time. The chapter ends by considering 'complicated mourning'; how we can know when this really exists, and when, sometimes, this diagnosis may result from a judgmental attitude governed by societal 'norms'.

A historical perspective on the study of the state of bereavement

The Oxford English dictionary (Second Edition, 1989) states that the common root of the words 'bereavement' and 'grief' is *reave*, which is derived from the old English word *reafian*: to plunder, spoil or rob. This gives us a pictorial sense that when someone is bereaved, something of value has been taken from that person against his or her will. There is a sense of abruptness, and the feeling that things have been left spoiled.

The clinical study of reactions to loss began in the early twentieth century with Freud (1913, 1917, & 1929). Prior (1989) describes this as the start of the normalising and medicalising of grief and sorrow. She goes on to say,

> ...these ideas contrast quite markedly with those of the nine-teenth century in which grief, although it was sometimes viewed as a cause of insanity, was never interpreted as itself pathological. Grief, if anything, was a condition of the human spirit or soul rather than of the body, and in that sense it could neither be normalised nor medicalised. (p. 133)

Freud gave the term 'mourning' to the behavioural and emotional changes that occur in a person following a significant death. Bowlby (1960) used the term at first to refer to the wide variety of reactions to loss; later he argued that there was a difference between grief and mourning. He defined mourning as the public act of expressing grief, which he determined as being an individual's spontaneous response.

A later definition, which takes into account cultural, societal and personal variants, is that of Averill (1968). He stated that mourning is the conventional behaviour determined by the mores and customs of the society, whereas he sees grief as a set of stereotyped psychological and physiological responses. He views both grief and mourning as dependent on the history and circumstances of the bereaved individual.

Stroebe et al (1993) define the key concepts in the following way. Bereavement is the loss of a significant other person in one's life; this triggers a reaction we call grief, which is manifested in a set of behaviours we call mourning. Klass et al (1996) however, suggest that mourning may be the period in which the survivor learns to live with the paradox of allowing the deceased to still be a continued presence in one's life, whilst simultaneously allowing them to be a part of one's past.

Freud was interested in the differences and the similarities between grief and depression, and he offered one of the first definitions of normal and pathological grief (1917). Freud's only explanation for pathological grief was that there must be some ambivalence towards the person who had died. He believed that the aggressive component of the ambivalent state turned inwards, and thus caused depression. He also saw grief as a solitary process and did not recognize the value of talking and seeking support and comfort from others. Freud's key theory, as described by Payne et al (1999), recognises that people form loving attachments to other people. Love is conceptualised as the cathexis (attachment) of libidinal energy to the psychological representation of the loved person ('libidinal energy' being positive/loving feelings). When the loved person dies, the person's libidinal energy remains attached to thoughts and memories of the deceased. Freud believed that grieving throws up the dilemma between the need to relinquish the relationship with the deceased, in order that the libidinal energy may be invested in a new relationship, and a wish to maintain the bond with the love object.

In these days of 'evidence based practice', there are some who are quick to denigrate such psychoanalytic theory as having no confirmatory evidence (Shackleton 1984). However, not everything is measurable, and psychoanalysis relies upon analytic intuition, valuable in its own right. There is also debate over the value of concentrating on the task of relinquishing bonds to the lost 'love object', in order to facilitate grief, and whether this is really the purpose of grief at all (Klass et al 1996). This will be discussed in more detail later in the chapter. It is of historical interest to note that later in Freud's life, when he experienced the death of his daughter and also that of his young grandson, his own experience of grief did not support his theoretical model. His notion of 'relinquishing the relationship' was something he was unable to do. However, this personal experience never influenced his written theories on this subject. We glimpse his personal experience of grief in a letter written to his friend Ludwig Binswanger after hearing of the death of Binswanger's son.

> Although we know that after such a loss the acute sense of mourning will subside, we also know we shall remain inconsolable and will never find a substitute. No matter what may fill the gap, even if it be completely filled, it nevertheless remains something else. And actually this is how it should be. It is the only way of perpetuating that love which we do not want to relinquish. (Freud 1961, p. 239)

What remains of importance to us is that Freud's early ideas stimulated interest in this previously neglected area, and provided the foundation upon which many other practitioners and researchers could build their own theories of grief. Klein (1940), for example, extended the theme of pathological grief. She asserted that all grief is, in a sense, pathological, insofar as it resembles the manic-depressive state, although for most people this is transitory. Many other studies also involved empirical surveys of the bereaved. The main works of this kind are that of Lindemann (1944), Marris (1958) Bowlby (1960, 1963, 1973) and Parkes (1965, 1972, 1975).

Lindeman (1944) held a series of psychiatric interviews with one hundred and one relatives of people killed either in the Boston Coconut Grove fire (N=13) or in the war (N=88). He concluded from this that grief was a syndrome that consisted of five components:

1 somatic disturbance
2 preoccupation with the image of the dead
3 guilt
4 hostility
5 disorganized behaviour

He also identified two patterns of abnormal grief: delayed grief, which may last for many years, and distorted grief. He named some of the manifestations of distortion as being: social isolation, hypochondriacal development of the dead person's symptoms, psychosomatic illness and manic over-activity. He said about grief work that it is the '... emancipation from the bondage of the deceased, readjustment to the environment...and the formation of new relationships.' (1944 p. 143) He also stated that the bereaved will have to express sorrow and a sense of loss, and that they will have to verbalize their feelings of guilt.

Lindeman's contribution is important because it was the first research in which duration and intensity of grief had been considered. He also acknowledges the importance of verbal expression, and highlights changes in social functioning. It is important, however, to note that some of the features put forward by Lindemann as abnormal grief, such as social withdrawal and hostility, were subsequently found by Parkes (1971) to be universal. As Shackleton (1984) says,

> Perhaps the most useful aspect of Lindemann's work is not the theory, but the encouragement he has given to the continued use of surveys of a general population of bereaved people.
>
> (p. 161)

In 1958, Marris built on Freud's theories as put forward in *Mourning and Melancholia* (Hogarth 1917/1961), but also used some of the findings of his own research (semi-structured interviews with seventy-two widows). He adds a cathartic approach to grief work, which is not dissimilar to that of Lindemann; however, he suggests that grief exists in a certain quantity, and must be released. He also stresses the importance of funerals. In 1974, Marris put forward a new theory of his own, leaving behind Freud's original theories. Marris cited bereavement as one example of major life change, and states that reactions to it can serve as a model to understand reactions to other major life changes such as marriage, moving house or being colonised. According to this theory, death is an 'irretrievable loss of the familiar' (in Shackleton 1984, p.163), which normally allows 'grown people to interpret and assimilate their environment' (ibid). This loss of predictability has a massive impact on the individual because:

> ...the impulse to defend the predictability of life is a fundamental and universal principle of human psychology... without continuity, we cannot interpret what events mean to us...(and) we could not survive even for a day if our physical environment were not predictable.   (in Shackleton 1984, p.163)

Marris describes two conflicting states which emerge at a time of bereavement. One is a wish to return to the time before the death, and the other is an impulse to deny or forget the whole issue. Recovery depends on working out the conflict between these two opposing wishes. He describes abnormal grief as occurring when the conflict is never resolved.

The evidence that Bowlby (1973) used for his thinking on attachment, separation and loss is derived from the descriptive work of Lindeman and Marris, and is also influenced by psychoanalytic theory from which he adopted ideas about predetermined biological patterns of instinctive behaviour, such as sucking and crying. Descriptions of separation reactions in animals, and the concept of imprinting, which Lorenz (1966) observed in geese, impressed Bowlby. His own clinical work with young people who had been displaced or orphaned during the second world war, and the work of the Robertsons on separation reactions in infants and young children also inspired him. All these aspects combined to influence the formulation of his theories. He believed grief to be an instinctive, universal response to separation, with the function of promoting union.

Bowlby's attachment theory emphasizes the biological, rather than the psychological, function of grief. He believed that in order to ensure the survival of new-born babies, both mothers and their infants have evolved a biological need to stay in constant contact with each other. He noted that the responses of grieving adults were similar to those of young children following the loss of their mothers. He noted three successive stages of distress when children are separated from their mothers: protest, despair and detachment. The protest stage functions to retrieve the lost person, and is characterized by searching, pining, restlessness, crying, anxiety and anger (particularly with the mother on her return). When the child's mother fails to return, the protest stage shifts to a stage of despair, char- acterised by the cessation of active searching and a move towards apathy and disorganised behaviour. Beyond this, the third stage is detachment; an apparent indifference of the infant to his environment.

On the basis of this attachment theory, Bowlby understood grief and mourning following bereavement to be a form of separation anxiety; his original theory developed to become a four-phase model. He was careful to emphasize that it was not a straightforward progression through four discrete phases. There would be some overlapping between phases, and people might move backwards and forwards between them, although it was anticipated that with time, most people would move through all phases. Bowlby went on to collaborate with Parkes. They influenced the development of each other's ideas, and jointly developed a phase model of grief (Bowlby & Parkes 1970) as well as continuing to develop their own independent work.

Payne et al (1999) write that Bowlby's theory (1980) made a number of important points:

- Grief responses are triggered by the loss of an attachment figure
- The closer and stronger the attachment, the more intense and enduring the distress of grief
- That during 'grief work', people cognitively redefined themselves and their situation, and that this was a necessary process of realising and reshaping internal representations to align them with changes that have occurred

Bowlby also interpreted pathological grief through attachment theory and made assumptions that it was connected to childhood experiences.

He hypothesised that there were three disordered forms of attachment in childhood that could increase vulnerability following bereavement: anxious attachment, avoidant attachment and disorganized attachment. (These will be referred to in more detail in Chapter 3).

As has been mentioned, Parkes' theory was influenced by Bowlby, with whom he worked closely. Parkes' theory differs in that he uses his own extensive data. He also gives a greater emphasis to the bereaved person's cognitive model of the world and to interventions; that is, work such as counselling which may occur with a bereaved person in order to support them through complex grief. He proposed that bereavement is a psychosocial transaction (Parkes 1971), which he describes as a '..complex interweaving of psychological and social processes' (1988 p. 53). There are similarities between Parkes' theory and that of Marris, in that they both believe that loss and bereavement challenge a person's assumptive world (the way the person has always assumed their life to be). Parkes' theory differs from Marris' views in that he suggests that one of the central tasks facing a bereaved person is to integrate the changes created by loss into a new or adapted assumptive world.

Payne et al (1999) describe Parkes' central idea in the following way. At a time of bereavement, individuals are required to modify or change their ways of being in the world that were functional before the loss, but are now meaningless or redundant without the deceased. Parkes proposed that there is a period of disorganisation, in which people discover that they can no longer continue to function as they did before the bereavement. He describes this as contributing to the distress and disruption of early bereavement. He suggests that people are resistant to change, but that they have to acknowledge the loss and the need for change before the demanding process of adapting can occur. Adapting would include the creation of new roles and identities for the bereaved person, as well as for their relationship with the deceased, including elements of identification with the deceased (which may include developing skills or interests that they may have had when alive). Parkes describes the outcome of successful grieving as gaining a new identity, that integrates the deceased into the life story of the survivor.

Like Bowlby, Parkes (1965) characterised grief as disease in his early work. His view at this time was that grief was one of the only mental disorders whose cause was known, and whose outcome was usually predictable. He pointed out that because grief presented with all the discomfort and loss of function associated with mental disorder, it must therefore be a mental illness.

By 1975 however, he had somewhat moderated this view, and was now of the opinion that only abnormal grief could be seen as illness.

Marris (1986, 1992) went on to develop his original ideas, and one important element that became central to his theory was the notion that grief was mastered by taking what was fundamentally important in the relationship with the deceased, and assimilating it into the new life without them. The importance of this, as Payne et al (1999) state, is that this contrasts with psychoanalytic and attachment theories and phase models of grief, all of which emphasise the need to sever emotional ties with the deceased. Marris' observations about the continuing importance of the meaning of the relationship with the deceased have been confirmed by research (Silverman 1986; Shuchter and Zisook 1993; Marwit and Klass 1995).

Phase or stage models

From Lindemann (1944) onwards, most theorists have developed models of grief which followed a general pattern that could be subdivided into 'stages' or 'phases', with the common view that the bereaved needed to 'work through' their grief in order to 'recover'. These phases may include some or all of the following: numbness, denial, yearning, anger, guilt, despair, disorganization and recovery.

These models have proved useful for practitioners in providing a description of the major themes of grief over time. However, there is always a danger that they are interpreted too literally, and may be used as a model as to how people 'should' respond. Although it has always been made clear by theorists that the stages are not a linear process, this may at times be forgotten. In addition to the 'stages' models of grief as a reaction to bereavement, Kubler-Ross (1969) developed a five-stage model of the grief of terminally-ill people as a response to their illness.

Current thinking has challenged these models, defining the grief process as so individualized and variable, and involving so many different facets of the bereaved person, that 'attempts to limit its scope or demarcate its boundaries by arbitarily defining grief are bound to fail' (Shuchter and Zisook 1993, p. 23). There are also challenges to the theory of recovery. Wortman and Silver (1989) suggest that for some people, grieving may continue for a number of years without it becoming 'complicated'. Payne et al (1999) state that few studies have followed people for more than two years, so it is difficult to know how long 'normal' grief should last. They add that it may be argued that loss changes people such that they are never the same again. This does not mean that they are psychologically damaged; in fact, it can mean that they may become more aware of their own resourcefulness, and also more conscious of the support network that exists around them.

Worden (1982, 1991) refined the 'stage' models, and drew on earlier concepts, (such as Freud's) that 'grief work' needed to be gone through before an adjustment could be made. He developed a four-task model of grief, which has been very influential and is used by many bereavement workers today. I suspect its popularity has been due to its focus on activity, or 'work to be done', which people can be guided through. This can give people working in this field apparent clarity over a process, which as we have seen, is not clear at all.

The four tasks are as follows:

1 To accept the reality of the loss
2 To work through the pain of the grief
3 To adjust to the environment without the deceased
4 To emotionally relocate the deceased and move on with life
   (Worden 1991, pp. 10-18)

New models of grief

Two models that look at grief in a multi-dimensional way, rather than the linear approach suggested by the earlier models, are Le Poidevin's seven dimensions of loss and that devised by Shuchter and Zisook (1993), which has six dimensions.

Le Poidevin's model remained unpublished at her untimely death in 1989; she had developed it while working with Parkes at St Christopher's Hospice in the early 1980s (see Parkes et al 1996). Her model is helpful in that it prompts enquiry from the bereavement worker into many areas of the bereaved person's circumstances, which may have been overlooked ordinarily, or been assumed known. It enables a much fuller picture to be drawn up of the meaning of this particular loss, for this particular person, at this particular time (see Chapter 6). The dimensions Le Poidevin considered were: emotional, social, physical, lifestyle, practical, spiritual and identity.

The dimensions of loss

Dimensions	Description
Emotional: strong emotions are usual	How comfortable is the individual with their emotional response? Do they believe in emotional control or are they at ease with expressing feelings?
Social: loss is experienced within a social network; it may cause changes in status and in role	What has been the impact on other members of the social network? What quality of support is available? What changes in status or role have to be negotiated?
Physical: physical symptoms are common	What has been the impact on physical health?
Lifestyle: loss may lead to major changes in lifestyle such as having to move houses or cope with financial difficulties	Has loss caused changes in lifestyle?
Practical: loss may affect the ability to cope with the practicality of everyday life such as cooking, shopping, self-care, child care and housework	How are everyday practicalities being managed?
Spiritual: loss may cause people to question their beliefs about the world and lead to a loss of meaning and purpose	In what ways has bereavement affected religious or other spiritual belief systems? What meaning has been ascribed to the loss?
Identity: loss may affect identity, self-esteem and feeling of self-worth	To what extent has loss affected the individual's self-concept and self-esteem?

Table 5.2 from Loss and Bereavement by Sheila Payne. Open University Press, 1999, p.84. Reprinted with kind permission of Open University Press and Professor Sheila Payne

The six dimensions outlined in the later model proposed by Shuchter and Zisook are: emotional and cognitive responses, coping with emotional pain, the continuing relationship with the deceased, changes in functioning, changes in relationships and changes in identity.

A significant development in this field has been the Dual Process Model (Stroebe and Schut 1999). These writers recognized that avoiding grief has its place at times, in adjusting to the state of bereavement. They acknowledge that it is important for bereaved people to take time off from the overwhelming roller-coaster of emotions that grief can be. Their framework builds on traditional models, particularly Worden's tasks of grief, but it introduces a second more pro-active concept - oscillation between coping behaviours. Stroebe and Schut propose that there are two aspects involved in adapting to bereavement: *loss orientation* and *restoration orientation*. Loss orientation encompasses all the traditional aspects of grief work, whereas restoration orientation includes mastering the tasks and roles undertaken by the deceased, making lifestyle adjustments, coping with everyday life, building a new identity without the deceased, and seeking distractions from painful thoughts. The central point to this model is the oscillation between the two states, both of which are necessary for adjustment. The degree and emphasis on each approach will vary for each individual. As Payne et al (1999) state, ' The model implies that judgments about the way a bereaved person is coping should not be made too quickly' (p. 86).

However, for all the advancements in new models and theories, Klass et al (1996) in their book, *Continuing Bonds* (Taylor & Francis), state that 'clinicians and researchers need to give up the hope of understanding grief in the context of a neat, orderly package that follows a single set of rules' (p. 351). They describe the complex and multi-dimensional process of mourning as being essentially a unique individual phenomenon, which encompasses the bereaved person incorporating the deceased into their lives while, at the same time, redefining themselves in the present. They share the belief that the continued bond with the deceased is a healthy part of the survivor's ongoing life, and that it may continue for the survivor's entire lifetime.

Complicated mourning

Pathological grief (Freud 1917, Parkes & Weiss 1983, Raphael 1984, Stroebe & Stroebe 1987) or abnormal grief (Worden 1982) now tends to be termed 'complicated mourning' or 'complicated grief'. The former terms were laden with judgements, and, as Klass et al (1996) point out, these states were not defined by research or clinical experience, but were based on the cultural values from which those models of grief emerged. So it was common (and still is to a certain extent) for someone's grief to be labelled as pathological if it was seen to be excessively intense and/or lasting for a prolonged period, or if it was too short and there appeared to be an absence of reaction. These diagnoses took no account of the particular individual circumstances, such as relationship to the deceased, spiritual, cultural and family belief systems, or social and environmental factors.

The concept of complicated mourning differs from this in that rather than conclusions being based upon frameworks such as timescale, or concepts such as the ability to sever the bond with the deceased, they are drawn from considering problems for the person in the here-and-now. These might include issues such as not being able to move forward with the rest of one's life, or difficulties in building other relationships. These problems may be linked to *complexities* in the person's continued relationship to the deceased, perhaps to do with difficulties in the social environment that surrounds the bereaved person in their daily lives, or they may have more deeply-seated psychological roots. These issues become of serious significance in the assessment, understanding and support of people with learning disabilities.

Resolution of grief

The phase models suggest that there will be an end point to the work of grief; that there is an adjustment to, or a resolving of, all the issues of bereavement. More recent theorists contest this. They state that mourning is an on-going process, which may or may not have an ending, and that the time-scale is unique to the individual and their circumstances. Payne et al (1999) suggest that grief may not therefore have a definite end-point which marks recovery. People may adapt to new roles and regain their interest in life. But they add, as Silverman (1986) also points out, in doing so, '..people don't give up the past, they change their relationship to it' (p. 7).

Rubin (1996) gives a new definition to resolution in terms of mourning. He states:

Resolution is the process that supplements and continues on beyond adaptation and/or coping with loss. The connections to the representations of the deceased and to the memories of the deceased continue on across the life-cycle.

(in Klass et al 1996, p. 352)

In the following chapter, I will examine the way in which society has historically excluded people with learning disabilities to the extent that, as Todd (2002) describes it, - 'they have been too eagerly treated as without culture, and, therefore, already dead' (p. 228). It is important to have an understanding of both the process of grief and the effect of this social exclusion, in order to grasp a full sense of the impact of bereavement upon people with learning disabilities.

Disability and society's death wish

Our society devalues the lives of people with learning disabilities. We even have difficulty in naming this group of people, reflecting, perhaps, the fear and disturbance that disability throws up for individuals and for society generally. It is important to remember that this is the backdrop against which all people with learning disabilities live and at whatever conscious level, the rejection and isolation imposed by society will have impact on them, particularly at a time when close bonds are broken through bereavement. Chapter 2 thus provides an exploration of this rejection, and concludes with an account of the hospitalisation of a young man with profound learning disabilities. This man's story contains many relevant elements that highlight the themes of the chapter.

In this book a large variety of terms have been used to describe people with 'learning disabilities', which is the term I choose to use (it is the word used within the UK Department of Health, and currently I feel the most accurate description). The current term used in USA is 'Intellectual Disability'. Where I refer to certain periods in history, I use the relevant historical term such as 'mental handicap', or 'feeble minded'. The term currently preferred by the self-advocacy movement is 'learning difficulty'.

The whole naming debate can become a very heated one. Through the centuries there have been many words used to name people with learning disabilities. Sinason (1992) states that no human group has been forced to change its name so frequently. She goes on to describe what happens as the currently favoured labels become outdated faster and faster, and often end up as words used to insult or hurt, as a process of euphemism.

'Euphemisms, linguistically, are words brought in to replace the verbal bedlinen when a particular word feels too raw, too near a disturbing experience' (Sinason 1992, p. 39-40).

There is an enormous taboo within our society towards disability, perhaps stemming from our own childhood fears of difference. Children often demonstrate their need to conform. They may have first-hand experience of the disadvantages of being the one who is different by being on the receiving end of bullying. To be 'very' different, that is to be visibly different through the manifestation of a disability, will often result in the child becoming segregated from peers long before this happens formally through the use of specialised services. These experiences must have an effect on the psyche of the individual with a learning disability and also on their family, influencing how members of the family relate to one another.

Many additional stresses are placed on the relationships within families where there is a member with a disability (Bicknell 1983). This process begins even before birth; from the moment of conception a new human life is under threat if not proven to be 'perfect'. Tests carried out in early pregnancy, such as the amniocentesis, are done with the intention of offering parents the option of eliminating the 'imperfect' baby. Valerie Sinason in her seminal work, *Mental Handicap and the Human Condition* (Tavistock 1992), highlights the death-wish our society harbours towards people with disabilities, and considers the impact of this on people with learning disabilities. Parents 'to be' may find themselves in the situation of having to choose very hurriedly whether to agree to terminate a pregnancy or not, having not been fully conscious of the process they were embarking upon when they first agreed to amniocentesis tests. Tests like these are society's inheritance from the eugenics movement, which strove to eliminate 'imperfection'. Eugenics is a term first used in 1883, meaning to strengthen a biological group (such as the human race) on the basis of hereditary worth (see further on in this chapter). This was one of the theories that led to many people with learning disabilities spending so many years of their lives in long stay hospitals, as it was socially perceived that some control over segregation of the sexes could be maintained inside these institutions. Eugenics has been presented as having a scientific basis; however as Marks (1999) states:

...the premise that it is a good idea to prevent certain citizens from procreating, even if accepted, would not necessarily have any effect on the gene pool. Further, even if it were possible to remove certain hereditary impairments from the gene pool, we might find that protective functions against certain illnesses (associated with the impairments) would be lost through selection.   (p. 34)

Some of the ideas left over from eugenics still appear to inform medical practice today; for example, we can see these principles continued currently with the mapping of the human genome (Clark, A. 2000). In his foreword to *Considered Choices* (BILD 2001) a book about the new genetics, Tom Shakespeare writes:

Understanding genetics enables scientists to understand diseases and, potentially, to develop therapies and drugs to alleviate conditions. In the future this will lead to better treatments for cancers, hypertension and a range of everyday problems. When there is no treatment for a disease, the major application of genetics will be in prenatal testing and selective termination of pregnancy.... these practices need to be introduced gradually, and with extreme caution.   (p. 4)

He goes on to say:

Social information about what it is like to be disabled - particularly information from disabled people themselves and their families - is as important in making these choices as genetic or clinical information.   (ibid)

And yet I have never heard of a family which, when faced with the dilemma of a positive test result, has been offered this sort of balanced information on which to form their decision. The personal views of the professional staff involved all too often influences the stance that they take in supporting families to make a choice (Helm et al 1998). Cooley et al (1990) compared the reactions and perceptions of mothers and medical professionals towards a film about Down syndrome. The results showed that:

...almost half of the genetic counsellors believed that the problems outweighed the benefits of parenting a child with Down syndrome, whereas 94% of the mothers and 83% of the nurses believed that the benefits prevailed. In addition, medical professionals were more likely to assume that mothers will want to terminate a pregnancy after a prenatal diagnosis of Down syndrome....

(Helm et al 1998, p. 55)

Parents who refuse such tests, or on receiving results showing that their baby may be born disabled choose to continue with the pregnancy, are often greeted with judgmental attitudes (Helm et al 1998). A mother of two children with learning disabilities describes how people often ask her: *"Couldn't they (the medical profession) have warned you or told you about your second child?"* (Picton 2001, p. 45). The implication is that if the mother had known about her baby's condition, she would surely have terminated the pregnancy. She reports that she and her husband were often made to feel that they had produced 'drains' on society. This same mother states how the dilemmas thrown up by the use of genetic screening leaves parents with guilt about their innermost feelings, and accords their children a very questionable value.

Some parents report their distress at the way in which the news of their baby's disability was broken to them. A father who wrote a book about his learning disabled son says, 'The reason I eventually wrote about him was because I felt from my own experience that parents of children were not always treated with understanding and sensitivity' (Hannam 1999, p. 29). He interviewed twenty-four other parents and found that in many ways their experiences had been similar. He described how 'much of the advice which had been received they found not only to be useless, but had hurt them deeply' (ibid). Other parents have written of the lack of support available to them. One such father wrote:

People were sympathetic but there was no support offered from professional counsellors to deal with all those feelings of self-deprecation; the guilt and anxiety. I was floundering in deep water and any lifeline seemed to be beyond reach. Add to this the uncertain explanations given by professionals, who were more than evasive. We have been left to constantly search for a rational explanation of our son's handicaps, knowing that this question might never be answered and may haunt us for the rest of our lives.   (Rendall 1997, p.78)

Parents report that the way in which the diagnosis is given to them is crucial, as it will have profound implications for the way in which the parents themselves respond and cope in the long term (Rendall 1997, Helm et al 1998).   The responses of parents to the birth of a child with a disability will also be influenced by whether they have received a prenatal diagnosis, or whether the diagnosis is not discovered until after the birth or even sometimes much later on. Parents who have been given the news prenatally will have made a conscious decision to keep their baby, and will have had time to adjust to the news.

Bicknell (1983) likens parents' responses to the news of their child's disability to that of a bereavement response. She quotes a mother of a baby born with spina bifida as saying, *"Do you know, when I was told that my baby was handicapped, something died in me."* (p. 167) Bicknell says this is the mourning for the loss of the perfect child. She describes how family members may grieve at different rates and therefore be at different stages within the grieving process at different times (see Chapters 1 & 3). This can put a huge strain on the family. Grandparents may work through their grief at a much slower rate than parents. Siblings may find themselves having to work through their grief for a second time when they reach adolescence in order to come to terms with the situation; since, at each new stage of development, a child will continue to work on and incorporate their understanding of, and their feelings connected to, earlier losses. Each parent may work through things at a different pace and be out of synch with each other's needs. Bicknell (1983) describes maladaptive responses to the 'bereavement response', depicting how families can get 'stuck' at various stages. For example, parents may become stuck in denial of their child's disability and try to find second and third opinions, often travelling to other countries and spending large amounts of money in the hope that they can reverse the diagnosis or find a miracle cure.

It may not be true that all parents mourn a 'perfect child', held in mind throughout the pregnancy. Some parents, perhaps, do not have a preconceived idea of how their baby will be; these parents might be open to greeting their baby in whatever way it arrives into the world. But for those who did not feel like this immediately, the tension between initial disappointment and eventual love for the child must create enormous guilt for parents.

The response of our society to disability does not make the news any easier to bear. The society in which we live places a high value on beauty, intelligence, independence, youth, and wealth, all elements important in our drive towards perfection. It can seem that without 'perfection', a life is written off as being worthless. Professionals will often focus on what limitations there will be for the baby, rather than what possibilities there are. Marks (1999) describes our society as narcissistic, a culture in which people strive for 'independence' and 'perfection'. She goes on to say that: '… the parts of the self that are unacceptable in a normalising culture' (such as bodily imperfection and dependency which we all experience in varying degrees). '… are kept outside conscious awareness and come to be split off and projected onto those who have been socially constituted as damaged' (p. 21). In other words, the bits of ourselves that we do not like, we seek out in others, in order that we can point a finger elsewhere and deny their existence in our own lives.

The message given by society is that it is a tragedy or a personal burden to have a child with a disability, and if it can be avoided, then there is an unspoken moral duty to do this (Loach 2003). What effect must this have on the parents of newly born babies with disabilities? And what effect must this have on people with learning disabilities as they grow up? To quote Marks again:

> It is often assumed that people with learning difficulties are oblivious to society's pity, hatred, and even death wishes towards them. They are seen to lack the 'emotional intelligence' or sensitivity possessed by 'normal' people. Yet the awareness of and concerns about amniocentesis, which often only emerge after several months in a therapy group, indicate that people with learning difficulties *are* aware of the value accorded to them.   (1999 p. 46)

On hearing the news that she was to become an aunt, Clare, a woman with mild learning disabilities, initially responded by becoming very excited. This changed rapidly, and as the birth grew nearer, Clare became increasingly concerned as to whether the baby would be born 'alright.' This demonstrated an awareness of her own disability, and the effect it has on others as well on her own life, but also perhaps an insight into the reality that babies may be killed off if they are not 'right'. Clare would have been aware of her family discussing the pregnancy and the various screening procedures. What thoughts must she have had about her own disability, and her family's response to her own birth?

Another woman with learning disabilities who was taking part in a workshop about genetics called 'Difference and Choice,' gave her perspective on the scientists' quest to perfect society through genetic screening:

> People with learning difficulties are different to other people. We get picked on - others make fun of us. People shout out in the street sometimes. Black people with learning difficulties get picked on even more. People with learning difficulties should be treated fairly and not discriminated against. Scientists should find the gene that makes people pick on those who are different. Then our lives would be better.
>
> (Howarth et al 2001, p. 39)

Linda Ward, from the Norah Fry Research Centre, Bristol, UK, (which aims to improve the quality of life for people with learning disabilities through research) says that if as a society we were really serious about reducing impairments, if we truly wish to strive for a better and healthier society, then we would need to look beyond the genes of disabled people. She says:

> We know that disabling conditions are not always, even mostly, the product of genetic 'disorders' alone, but are frequently *a product of the interplay between genetics and the environments in which people live and their experiences."* (My italics)
>
> (Ward 2001, p. 13)

It would seem pertinent at this point to mention the social model of disability. This model was formulated by activists and scholars in the UK, and locates disability not in an impaired or malfunctioning body, but in an excluding and oppressive social environment (Marks 1999). Barnes, quoted by Marks (ibid) defines disability as 'the loss or limitation of opportunities to take part in the normal life of the community on an equal level with others due to physical and social barriers.' (Barnes 1994, in

Marks 1999, pp. 79-80). This perhaps comes close to what the woman in the workshop wants us to hear.

Sinason (1992) draws our attention to social history, helping us to see how it provides communities and individuals with a sense of developmental progression. She reminds us how knowledge and learning have always been linked to the great religions, and that, paradoxically, this connection has played a part in defining handicap. 'For if no-one can read or write, then only those with the most severe handicaps will be noticed' (Sinason 1992, p. 57). Marks (1999) defines industrialisation as being the point in history when defining normality became a concern. She writes that: 'Mechanised production required a uniform work force, who could perform similar tasks, and work was not organised to cater for the range of intellectual and bodily differences between people' (p. 80). She quotes Finkelstein (1980) who identified three stages of historical development, which have had an impact on people with disabilities. The first phase he defines as feudal society, characterised by agricultural production or small-scale industry. He states that most people with impairments could contribute in some way and would therefore have been included in social life. The second phase was the move to industrialisation and factory production. This is when people with disabilities began to be excluded from productive labour. This type of work needed more speed and discipline and was not as flexible as the smaller scale work; this meant that anyone who could not keep up with the 'norm' was left out.

The third phase that Finkelstein identified, and views as just beginning, is one in which people with disabilities will be liberated by the introduction of new technologies. This perspective may be rather over-optimistic, but it would be good to believe there may be something in it.

Sinason (1992) quotes the Lord Brian Rix (President of the British charity Mencap) as he warns us against having any illusions that things were better in the past, or even in less developed countries where society is not as dependent on literacy. 'I want us to be aware of the enormous problems in third-world countries where people with a mental handicap are rejected and marginalised today in their own rural communities' (1990 p. 14).

A few years ago I had the opportunity to travel to Zimbabwe to work as a training consultant with a learning disability organisation there. What was immediately and painfully obvious was the huge gulf between the wealthy culture in which I live, and the poverty that I witnessed in Africa. The learning disability schools and day-centres that I saw were poorer than I could ever have imagined, without having seen them first hand. The level of disability in the schools was mixed, but mainly in the mild to moderate continuum, with a few classes for students who had severe disabilities. The level of disabilities in the day-centres was mild to moderate. One of the things that struck me as so different between our two cultures was that in all the activities carried out with people with learning disabilities, the emphasis was strongly on learning practical skills. In the schools, a large part of the curriculum focused on skills such as cooking, growing vegetables, cereal and fruit, and looking after live-stock. In the day-centres, these skills were important as well, but these centres also had to fund themselves. They were run as small industrial centres with crafts such as coffin making, weaving and metal work. All these items were sold to local businesses, and the centres also ran a small shop selling the fresh produce.

During the trip I was taken to visit a hospital, where many people with learning disabilities lived. Despite the hard work of the professionals there, the conditions were shocking. The hospital was overcrowded, with mattresses crammed side-by-side in every available space; even the corridors and walkways outside in the scorching sun had people lying or sitting in them. There seemed to be little opportunity for staff to even consider the psychological care of these people; they were simply existing. This population was mainly people with severe and profound learning disabilities. When I asked how people came to be at the hospital, I was told that many of them were found abandoned in the bush or townships. It made tragic but enormous sense to me that in a country as poor as this, if your offspring are unable to contribute to the family's existence in some way, then there might be little choice other than to abandon the child in order that he or she did not place a burden on a family which was already struggling to survive.

Recently, I have considered this again in the light of the depression that can occur in mothers after the birth of a child with a disability, in our own society. Perhaps depression could be seen as being an outdated inherited evolutionary response to the unnatural state of bonding with and nurturing of a child, which, in different circumstances, might have threatened the family's ability to survive at the most basic level. This is an unbearable thought, especially within the context of an affluent society where there is no real threat to a family's physical survival. However the unconscious perception of a mother may be that there is still an enormous and valid threat to her family's survival, but it is a threat to their psychological survival. We may no longer live in fear of death from starvation, but perhaps because of the removal of this threat, we are more aware of the psychological starvation people experience. The impoverished quality of life many people with learning disabilities are leading, due to a lack of emotional consideration and support, clearly amounts to such comparisons.

The legacy of eugenics

Francis Galton coined the term 'eugenics' in 1883. His ideas were based on his interpretation of Darwin's theory of natural selection. Whilst eugenics has come to be associated with the atrocities of the Nazi regime, at various other points in history it has been supported by some of the most progressive social reformers such as Marie Stopes, whose work on birth control was motivated by the theory. The first forced sterilisation of 'feeble minded' people was carried out in the early part of the twentieth century, in the USA (Kennedy, 1942; Kanner, 1942; Hubbard, 1997 as quoted by Marks 1999). By 1920, laws had been passed in twenty-five states leading to the compulsory sterilisation of the criminally insane and others considered genetically inferior. This continued in some states throughout the Second World War, and into the 1950s. By 1958, over sixty thousand American citizens had been forcibly sterilised (Hubbard, 1997 as quoted by Marks 1999). Euthanasia was also justified through governmental policies in Nazi Germany as a procedure by which to alleviate the perceived burden imposed upon society. Alongside the genocide of the Jewish people, thousands of disabled people were systematically murdered (Lifton 1986, Proctor 1988); this is less often referred to in accounts of the holocaust. When writing about the recent advances in the science of genetics, disabled writer and activist Agnes Fletcher says:

Many disabled people are anxious that the mass sterilisation and murder that occurred in the name of genetics in the early part of this century, which led to the extermination of people on the basis of other traits deemed hereditary, were not a Nazi anomaly but an extreme instance of a deep-seated hostility towards, and fear of, impairments.

(Fletcher 2001, p. 72)

No doctor was ever prosecuted for war crimes against disabled people (Gallagher 1990). As Marks (1999) writes, 'The implicit and pervasive nature of eugenic philosophy in Western society helps to explain some of the extreme violations carried out against disabled people in the twentieth century' (p. 35).

A subtle ghost of this thinking lives on in our so-called humane society today. We can still see second-rate health care offered to people with learning disabilities; practices such as cancer screening are rarely offered (Mencap 1998), and a report by the UK Department of Health highlights difficulties for people with learning disabilities in accessing a good enough service in hospitals due to their fear and distress. This is often caused through problems in communication (*Secondary health care for people with a learning disability*, UK Department of Health report 2000). Terminal illnesses are often diagnosed very late, and palliative care is rarely considered as an option. There seems to be an unspoken view within much of the medical profession that people with disabilities would be better off dead; this view holds particularly strongly if the person has a profound learning disability.

I have heard many sad and angry accounts of experiences when an individual with learning disabilities has become terminally ill. Almost without exception, the stories have contained themes of not being valued, not being understood and not being offered a fair service. Perhaps there is no conscious wish on behalf of medical staff to respond negatively towards patients with learning disabilities. But there is often fear and a lack of knowledge, and these can lead to ill-informed practice and defensiveness.

Paul, a young man of twenty-two, had a profound learning disability and severe scoliosis, which meant that the curve of his spine led to his rib cage pushing into his abdomen on one side. He weighed five stone and always had trouble taking his food, eventually receiving most of it in liquid form. Paul was admitted to hospital with severe dehydration because he had become unable to take fluids, and a chest infection was also suspected. Consider how shocking it may have been to mainstream medical staff to receive such a severely deformed and emaciated young man into their care, in such a critical condition. They would not have had experience of Paul's previous twenty-two years spent in loving relationships, enjoying many aspects of his life. All they were able to see were his damaged body and their own limitations at being able to communicate with him.

During his time in hospital the chest infection was never confirmed, but the main problem that Paul had in taking liquids became the focus of care. It became a concern that he might aspirate (take fluid down into his lungs) if he were given liquid by mouth. Paul was given a drip but this proved problematic, as he had very poor veins and the tube either fell out or had to be re-sited for fear of infection or the skin trying to heal over the tube. Each time it was harder and harder to find fresh suitable sites. On one occasion, Paul had to endure going for many hours without any liquid by drip, while a professional opinion was sought regarding re-siting.

His mother felt from the first moment that Paul was admitted to hospital that the staff had not been able to see the person behind the deformity and the emaciation of his body. She did not blame them, but she felt that this influenced the care he received, unconsciously if not consciously; sometimes care seemed to take longer to arrive than might have been necessary, for example. Paul's mother felt there was an unspoken "He'd be better off dead, poor thing" in the staff's attitude. Yet to her, her husband and the care staff who were with Paul night and day, it was clear that a lot of the time, Paul was in good spirits; he was lively and interactive. They all felt that Paul simply required the problem with taking liquid to be investigated, and, hopefully, dealt with.

The residential staff from Paul's house were on a twenty-four hour rota in the hospital, to ensure that there was always someone with him to help him mediate with this new environment, to give social and nursing care and also to support Paul's parents. Paul's mother later said that she could not have coped without the continuous support of the staff; she felt that the residential staff, she and her husband were like a team. She added that the continual attendance of the residential staff allowed her and her husband time to communicate with nursing and medical staff within the hospital, in order to ensure the best care was provided for Paul.

Paul had been admitted to a ward full of elderly people, which in this particular hospital meant darkening the ward for an afternoon sleep each day. This was completely inappropriate for Paul. Apart from anything else, he wanted to bang his tambourine and make his usual sounds; his normal form of communication. His parents eventually managed to get him moved to a side-room, and once he was moved, the residential staff transformed the room into the sort of sensory environment Paul had been used to at home and in his day-centre. They brought in items from home such as posters, fibre optics, streamers, things to bash and his C.D. player with his own music. Once word started to spread, staff came from all around the hospital to see the transformation of an ordinary side room into this magical place, which was of course Paul's usual environment.

There was an obvious interest in Paul and his room. Unfortunately the interest did not extend to linking up with his community care workers, of which there were a number involved; the speech and language therapist, the dietician and the physiotherapist, all of whom had known Paul nearly all his life. They all had a good knowledge of his physiology; they may well have held vital information, which could have been used to enable successful management of his needs whilst in hospital. Sadly, they were never contacted.

There was an extended medical debate about Paul's treatment, during which time his condition deteriorated. Eventually the hospital care team decided that they could do nothing more for Paul and his parents, and the decision was made to return Paul to the care home where he had lived for the last year. During the last seven days of Paul's life, he was cared for by the residential staff, nursing staff from the GP practice and by nurses from the local hospice. Paul's mother felt their interaction with Paul exemplified the care that should have been given to him whilst he was in hospital, in that they had regarded Paul as an individual in his own right with respect, dignity and compassion. He died surrounded by his friends, family and the staff who cared for him so much.

Paul's mother maintains that she could not have coped without the support of the residential staff; they continued to give her the strength to fight for Paul's life, and not to feel that she was fighting for a lost cause. The residential and nursing staff had continued to respond to Paul-the-person, whereas in the hospital environment, people did not seem to be able to see the individual, but only the problems. To those people who could read his signals, Paul had continued in his own way to be full of life. Paul's parent's were never given an answer to the cause of the condition which led to his eventual death. The question remains as to whether or not he was given due priority, or whether because of Paul's underlying learning and physical abnormalities, he was not given optimum care.

Paul's mother regrets that the specialist learning disability professionals from the community were not called upon to provide their knowledge and expertise, which she feels may have aided the hospital staff in their decision-making, and may have helped her to know what went wrong.

Something that stands out from the sad story above is the importance of the role of professionals other than the hospital team. The residential staff played an invaluable part in supporting Paul and his family, and as Paul's mother states, it would have been very useful to have had some input from the community learning disability team.

The role of the residential staff should be respected by hospital staff and family alike, and can be summarised as follows:

1 To be recognised as having a close relationship with the patient (often like family)
2 To have their specialist knowledge of the individual taken into account (communication, sensory needs, particular way to administer medication, how the patient seems in himself/herself, for example)
3 To make the medical environment conducive to the needs of the patient (bringing in familiar things, possibly adding sensory and interactive items)
4 To work in partnership with nurses and doctors (providing reports from other professionals speech therapists, physiotherapists, dieticians and so on)

In 1998 Linda McEnhill formed The National Network for the Palliative Care of People With Learning Disabilities in the United Kingdom (see Resources List). This is made up of partnerships between palliative care professionals, people working in learning disability services and carers. Its main aim is to encourage palliative and health care professionals and learning disability professionals to find positive ways of working in partnership. It came about through the recognition that people with learning disabilities were often not having access to the services that anyone else would expect when they were dying. The network carries the hope that the final days and weeks for terminally-ill people with learning disabilities could be spent in some comfort and dignity, just as other members of our society would hope for.

To conclude: society devalues people with learning disabilities, and as the title of this chapter states, it even has a death wish towards them. As Sinason (1992) suggests, there is a fine line between screening to prevent babies being born with a disability, and wishing people who have disabilities dead.

In the affluent West these prejudices should no longer apply. We can afford to recognise these outmoded fears for what they are, and instead be creating a more tolerant society. We are undergoing a slow but steady evolutionary development towards a society that is more able to tolerate diversity of ability.

In the last century the technological revolution has been extraordinary. We have computers that can perform many of the functions such as spelling and arithmetic with which people with learning disabilities have struggled. We have telephones, which can automatically remember numbers. These are examples of some of the aids that can enable people with learning disabilities to live independent and fulfilling lives. However, what still remains as a barrier are the attitudes of a disabling society, which results in insensitive and sometimes barbaric treatment of people with learning disabilities.

Chapter 3

Grief becoming complex

Klass et al (1996) describe how the positive value placed on autonomy, and the negative value placed on dependence in our culture, affects the prevailing way in which we understand grief. It will be in the light of this thought that I reflect upon the grief of people who may be more dependent than most. I examine research on childhood bereavement, in the hope that with deeper knowledge of the way in which we all build up our knowledge of mortality and the capacity to cope with grief, we may understand a little bit more about some of the complex and varied factors which can affect the grieving process for someone with a learning disability. Attachment theory contributes an important perspective from which to consider the relationships between a disabled child and their parents, particularly in light of the death of the parent. Finally, it is useful to think about some of the environmental factors surrounding someone with a learning disability, and how this may hinder a healthy grieving process.

Grief in childhood

If we are to try to understand the relationship between grief and learning disability, then it is necessary to examine how the capacity to mourn develops within normal childhood and to consider what issues may affect this development.

Today, most professionals are in agreement that children grieve. However, there is an ongoing debate as to what age this ability is acquired. Studies show contradictory evidence in the debate. The process of mourning is inherent to loss, and as Bowlby (1963) and the Robertsons (1953) report, it is present in even very young infants, on recognition of the loss (however temporary) of a parent. They claimed that children as young as six months experience grief reactions when separated from their mothers for long periods of time. Other views differ. Wolfenstein (1966) believed that the capacity to mourn was not reached until adolescence, whereas R. Furman took a more middle line by claiming that the capacity to mourn begins between three and a half to four years of age (1973).

Experiencing grief reactions is of course only one part of the process of mourning. It has been documented that there are three basic requirements for bereaved children to keep parental memories alive (Buchsbaum1996), and that these memories are necessary for mourning to occur (as stated in The Institute of Medicine Report 1984). These are:

• An understanding of the concept of death
• The ability to form a genuine attachment
• The possession of a mental representation of the attachment figure

These three factors will be explored in this chapter in relation to people with learning disabilities.

The concept of death

Understanding some of the more difficult concepts connected to death is complex. Worden (1996) states that 'The child's comprehension of death and the role this comprehension plays in the process of mourning is a major component in our understanding of childhood bereavement.' (p. 10). Many of the more abstract concepts of death, such as finality and irreversibility, will be related to the child's level of cognitive development (E. Furman, 1974; Piaget, 1954; Smilansky, 1987).

There are several different schools of thought on how children develop this understanding. Nagy (1948, 1959,) describes three distinct conceptual stages of childhood mourning but she does not believe that these begin until three years old. More recent researchers would say that some children develop a realistic understanding of death much earlier, depending on their life experience.

Kane (1979) carried out research on one hundred and twenty-two children of average intelligence to identify their understanding of death. She identified the main components of the concept of death based on previous literature, and used these as a basis for her questions. The components were:

Realisation	the awareness of death as a state of being, as something which happens
Separation	the location of the dead, for example in the sky, under the ground
Immobility	whether the dead are seen as active or inactive
Irrevocability	whether death is permanent or reversible
Causality	external or internal causes, for example gun or heart attack
Dysfunctionality	the person's ideas about the body functions of the dead apart from the senses
Universality	everyone dies
Insensitivity	whether a dead person can feel anything
Appearance	how someone may look when they are dead
Personification	death as a concrete thing, for example a bogeyman

Kane found that the components were acquired gradually, and that the process was consistent with Piaget's model of development. Perhaps our focus should be on the emotional response to separation, as reactions can be seen in children without any need for cognitive understanding. Bowlby (1967) and the Robertsons'(1953) early studies also seem to demonstrate that mourning is not dependent on understanding the concept of death, but on loss itself. Environmental and life experience are as much a factor as age in the development and gaining of knowledge and understanding in connection with mourning. Sula Wolff (1969) suggests that 'There is evidence that the harmful effects of bereavement are more often due to its long-term social and psychological consequences, and to the emotional reactions of the surviving parent, than to the impact of the death itself upon the child.' (p. 86).

From the above, we can conclude that cognitive understanding is less important than life experience and environmental factors for a child of any age coping with bereavement, including whether the surviving parent and/or anyone else is able to offer appropriate support at the time. The type of early attachment made is also important, and the ability to remember the deceased and whether the child is supported in doing this. We could make an assumption that these factors will be the same for an adult with a learning disability.

People with learning disabilities can remain disadvantaged in terms of acquiring knowledge or experience for their entire lives. Unlike children without disabilities, learning disabled children can continue to be shielded, protected or overlooked when people close to them die; indeed, this can happen throughout their adult lives as well. An added complication occurs when the loss is not acknowledged or is overlooked, as is so often the case both for children and people with learning disabilities. When this happens the grief process can become inhibited or complicated.

Understanding the development of the death concept in adults with learning disabilities

When we move from the literature on childhood bereavement, and begin to look at the research and literature on bereaved adults with learning disabilities, we see many similarities, with the addition of other complicating factors involving the role of services. The balance between cognitive understanding, life experience and the quality of support offered at the time of bereavement are still crucial factors. It is interesting to note that there is far less material on bereavement and people with learning disabilities than on childhood bereavement.

Bihm and Elliot (1982) suggest that it is the cognitive level (as defined by Piagetian tasks) rather than chronological age which determines the development of the concept of death in people with learning disabilities. However Lipe-Goodson & Goebel (1983) disagree, and found that an understanding of death appeared to depend on age and experience rather than intelligence. They concluded that this was similar to that normally developed in children, but that some adults with learning disabilities would never have a fully developed concept of death. McAvoy (1986) noted from his research that there was an apparent lack of understanding of the link between ageing and dying, and the fact that this was a natural part of the life cycle. This lack is likely to occur since people with learning disabilities often continue to be treated as children, and are perhaps unaware of the process of ageing until they begin to experience obvious signs in themselves and others.

It is not until about 1977 that we find any reference in the literature to evidence that people with learning disabilities grieve; possibly because historically it was thought that people with learning disabilities could not make emotional attachments.

Oswin made an important observation between about 1960 and 1976 when she was spending time visiting 'residential institutions for mentally handicapped children and adults' while researching her book *The Empty Hours* (Penguin 1971). She stated that she often met residents who had suffered the death of a close relative and had then been abruptly admitted to residential care, and how pitifully sad these people were. This led to the recommendation in her next book *Holes in the Welfare Net* (Bedford Square Press 1978) that some work should be done around this issue. She was instrumental in the next step, taken by the King's Fund in the form of a study group discussing bereavement and mentally handicapped people's grief, resulting in the paper *Bereavement and Handicapped People* (1989). Subsequently, the Rowntree Fund sponsored further work in the UK which led to Oswin's seminal work, *Am I Allowed to Cry?* (Sovereign Press 1991).

But the earliest clearly documented report that grief was being felt and expressed by people with learning disabilities is that of Emerson (1977). She found that fifty percent of the people referred to her because they had suddenly started to present with 'emotional and management difficulties' had experienced either the death or the loss of an individual close to them preceding the onset of the symptoms (see Chapter 4).

Kloeppel and Hollins (1989) state that:

> Limited ability to understand events and put them in appropriate context, combined with significant dependence, makes the mentally handicapped person particularly vulnerable to the uncertainties and insecurities normally associated with the death of a loved one.   (p. 34)

We begin to see how important the social environment around a grieving individual with learning disabilities is. It is often the quality of support given that determines how complicated or uncomplicated the grieving will be.

Oswin (1985) contributes to this thinking when she adds that people with 'mental handicap' may have additional special difficulties due to:

- Poor intellect and multiple disabilities, which may deny them the many social, verbal, auditory and visual opportunities of realising the death, that are available to more able people
- The failure of professionals and other people to recognise their normal grief reaction

• The inappropriate way in which their services are organized (p. 198)

She makes it clear that as professionals or family members, we need to consider some of the extra factors which may make it more difficult for someone with a learning disability to realise the actuality of the death.

However, research by Harper and Wadsworth (1993) highlights the point that although developmental understanding of death may be an important factor, they are unsure in what way it relates to the ability to work through a 'normal' mourning process. Their study shows that a surprisingly large percentage of the adults interviewed displayed an accurate comprehension of the irreversibility and universality of death, and acceptable and positive coping with loss despite limited cognitive and verbal expressive skills. They question whether this was related to the level of conceptual awareness, prior experience and belief (both secular and religious), existing support or some interactive combination of these. This research shows that it is important to consider the cognitive and emotional development, the life experience, the social environment and the belief system of an individual when considering the impact of the death of a significant other person. Many individuals with a profound learning disability for example, may not have the cognitive ability to understand some of the complex concepts of death, but they are still likely to have an emotional response to the loss of someone significant in their lives.

Oswin (1989) states that people who are 'severely multiply handicapped' may find it difficult to understand verbal explanations about their loss, and that their main comfort may be through being held and comforted or through being offered a familiar object that has some special meaning for them. Others more cognitively able may have a strong religious belief system that enables them to cope well; for others, there may appear to be almost an indifference to the loss. There may be several reasons for this. For example, many other functions within that person may be much slower, so it is likely that emotional response to loss may also be slow. However it may be something altogether different. Deutsch (1937) describes a possible hypothesis in her paper on the absence of grief; she says,

> …the phenomenon of indifference is due to the fact that the ego of the child is not sufficiently developed to bear the strain of the work of mourning and it therefore utilizes some mechanism of

narcissistic self-protection to circumvent the process.

(in Worden 1996, p. 70)

The development of the 'ego', the part of ourselves that is our sense of self, can often be hindered in people with learning disabilities for reasons ranging from organic damage to social and intrapsychic factors. One important factor to consider is the degree of dependency that the person has on others, as this will impact on their ego development. Children develop a more complete sense of themselves as they experience greater and greater autonomy and mastery of the world; when this is limited it can impact on psychological development. For the developing child with a learning disability, the extent to which they need support from other people in order to explore the environment and gain steps towards independence will affect their developing ego.

Attachment

Another major factor is the early attachment between parents and infant. This primary relationship affects all other relationships as well as the individual's sense of themselves. The first few days of a baby's life are a crucial time for parents and child to bond (Schaffer 1958, Ainsworth et al 1974, Bowlby 1979). John Bowlby's work on early relationships between parents and their infant children (1979) concluded that a healthily functioning attachment system exists to protect the child from harm or threat, and also provides a secure base from which the child can explore the environment. The relationship with the parent is the basis upon which the growing infant develops a sense of self and their model of relating to others. The mental health and emotional robustness of parents at the time of birth will affect this process, as will the surrounding environment.

When a baby is born with a disability, there are often obstacles standing in the way of the important process of child and parent bonding. Receiving news about their baby in such ways as have previously been described (Chapter 2) will be traumatic; parents may need to grieve for the 'perfect' baby that they didn't have. Many expectant parents will have developed a vision for their growing baby before it is born, and for most parents this will not include the presence of a disability. They will have to adjust themselves to a different vision of their own and their baby's future. They will have to cope with their own responses to this baby; whether they can see beyond the baby's disability and possible disfigurement, to family resemblance and other features on which new parents commonly linger with delight. They will have to cope with the responses of other family members, friends and professionals. The differing responses that the mother and father of the baby have from each other may put additional strains on their relationship. At the same time as having to deal with all these conflicting and possibly upsetting feelings and responses, the parents also have to nurture and respond to their baby's needs.

The mother in particular may become very depressed and withdraw from her child, or she may respond by becoming over protective. Either of these reactions will affect the bonding process, and consequently the developing child. These responses are likely to become established in the pattern of their relationship (see Chapter 4).

Bowlby (1979) and Ainsworth et al (1974) noted a variety of attachment styles; children who grow up with a healthy attachment model are able to depend upon and trust adults and also develop a perception of themselves as loveable. This is called a *Secure* attachment style. A child brought up by a parent who constantly discouraged or rejected the display of feelings may grow up to feel unloved; they are likely to develop an *Avoidant* attachment style. They may turn away from others when under threat, and in times of crisis, they may 'de-activate' attachment related behaviour by downplaying emotional responsiveness. They may grow up to feel unlovable, constantly provoking rejection. A third style evolves in those with inconsistent and unpredictable early care-giving, such as a child who may have experienced many separations from parents due to regular hospital stays in early years. Alternatively a parent may have given the child the message that they will not survive unless they stay very close to them, leaving the child with mixed feelings about relationships. These children tend to worry that others around them do not really care for them; they are difficult to please or placate and can often be viewed as clingy or needy. This is known as the *Ambivalent* attachment style. A depressed, emotionally unavailable parent, or an abusive parental relationship is likely to lead to a *Disorganised* style of attachment; this creates a paradox for the child, who is faced with a need to seek the proximity of the same adult who is also a source of danger, or who is unable to respond.

A child growing up with an over protective mother may not find it easy to relate to others, (this would be an *Ambivalent* attachment pattern) especially if the relationship with the mother has been quite exclusive.

This may make coping with group situations difficult, for example. It is painful to think of the adjustment an individual with this sort of relationship would have to make when his sole surviving parent dies, and he finds himself moved into a group home. The pattern set up will be one of exclusivity, of being special, of the whole world revolving around this individual. The relationship may be such that the child never has to state their needs as they are always met by the mother almost before the child becomes aware of them himself (see case study of John in Chapter 10).

At a time of bereavement the way in which we cope can determine whether we grieve healthily or not. The way in which we cope will, to some extent, be determined by how we relate to others around us and how they respond; this response will also be determined to some extent by our experience and our expectations set up within our primary relationships.

I met Timothy a few months after his mother had died. He lived in a group home for learning disabled people, and before that had lived for many years in a long stay hospital. The staff in the home described Timothy as selfish and bullying. They told me what little they knew of his history before he had come to live in the home. He had lived with his mother and sister up until his adolescence, when his mother had felt that she could no longer manage him. His father had left the family when Timothy was a baby, and had very little if any contact with him. The staff told me that his mother frequently visited him at the group home, right up until her death. They said that she would always arrive with a huge bag of sweets, which Timothy would grab from her as soon as she walked through the door. If his mother got out her cigarettes, he would grab the whole packet from her, light one up, and she would let him keep the rest. The staff said that Timothy bullied his mother, and that she had over indulged him and been frightened of him.

It struck me that perhaps this was a mother who had begun by being over-protective, perhaps from a desire to protect a disabled child from a cruel and rejecting world or perhaps from an overcompensation for her own feelings of rejection towards her child. Whichever it was, her child had become the 'Frankenstein' monster, out of control. As he became bigger and bigger, she had increasingly tried to appease him and he in turn had learned that he could control her more and more. This has left him a sorry legacy. He still expects the world to work in the same way and as it does not, he spends most of his life in conflict with others.

I have come across many similar stories to this one. Worden (1991) describes how important it is to take the nature of the relationship with the deceased into account, as this will determine how the person is grieved for. For this man and others like him, a part of grieving for his mother will be adjusting to the way the rest of the world treats him without his mother to buffer it for him.

The vignette above describes a rather frozen relationship between mother and son; it appears to have become stuck at the stage of toddlerhood, and not developed further in terms of boundary setting. This led to an enmeshed relationship, which has made it impossible for the man in question to mature and develop some autonomous sense of himself in relation to a broader social network. Tyson-Rawson (1996) states:

> The way in which human beings experience the world, and themselves, is shaped, moderated, and reciprocally influenced by the relational contexts within which they live. This network of relationships is primary in the development of the individual's understanding of the meaning of the death experience and the nature of the self.   (p. 125)

Keeping memories of the deceased alive

Buchsbaum (1996) offers some useful thinking on bereavement from a developmental perspective. One component that she stresses as an important contributing factor to a satisfactory outcome to a period of mourning is the use of memory. She reports that: 'memories appear soon after the occurrence of a death has been comprehended' (p. 113). She goes on to state:

> In this phase, memory serves as an anchor from which attachments to the deceased can gradually be relinquished... Memories of the deceased serve as an essential bridge between the world with and the world without the loved person.
>
>   (ibid)

It is significant to think about the function of memory generally when we are considering people with learning disabilities, as memory is something which some people may need support in developing and sustaining. It is important at a time of bereavement for supporters to enable the person to have mementoes and 'prompts' of the deceased person (for example, photos or items belonging to the deceased that may hold memories for the bereaved person), and to provide opportunities for reflection and memories in a sensitive manner. Buchsbaum (1996) goes onto describe the next phase after the acute phase of mourning as being a time when images of the lost person can start to be understood as part of the past. '…Entering consciousness at the command of the bereaved, providing a sense of consolation, continuity and inner enrichment' (p. 113).

A third occasion for the emergence of memories of the dead is when anniversaries occur, such as family events, birthdays and the period of time around the anniversary of the death. For someone with a learning disability who may have difficulty in reflecting on how they are feeling as they are supported in remembering the deceased, associations connected to an anniversary may be particularly strong. These memories and associations may arise more from a sense of the familiar feeling unfamiliar, rather than from a conscious anticipation of the absence. There may also be strong sensory reminders, such as the season of the year, particular foods or smells and so on. For example Christmas and other religious festivals can be a difficult time particularly for people who have lived in the family home prior to the bereavement. They may suddenly be hit with the reality that this Christmas is unfolding in a very different way to other Christmases, now that the deceased person is no longer here to do things the way that they have always been done in the past. It is important to be aware of, and sensitive to, these times for the person with learning disabilities, and to the meanings evoked for them, especially as they may not make the connection for themselves and may therefore 'act out', expressing their distress at the change through their behaviour.

The fourth mode of remembering Buchsbaum (1996) describes is when symbolic representations of the deceased finds an outlet in the creative process. This can be an important means of expression and also a link to the deceased. Creative ways of working have been used successfully as an intervention with bereaved people with learning disabilities (Blackman 1999, 2000, 2002, Read 1999 a 1999 b) (also see creative interventions in later chapters).

Buchsbaum also states, in reference to bereaved children (1996), that 'disruption of the child's continuous, taken-for-granted exchanges with the parent can result in an inner sense of fragmentation, confusion, and disjointedness.' (p. 115). This is extremely pertinent with regard to people who have grown up with a learning disability, and perhaps additional physical complications. There may well be a history of 'disrupted exchanges' prior to bereavement, with possible hospital stays, respite care, boarding school or a move into residential care in early childhood. With this history in mind, there may already be the sense of fragmentation and confusion described above, which can only be exacerbated by bereavement. It is important to note here that parental memories contribute to a bereaved child's personality development (Spitz 1957, Emde 1983, Mahler, Pine & Bergman 1975). This can inform us that it may be essential to provide means by which parental memory (in other words memories of the deceased parent), can be maintained and reflected upon in order to enable personal growth as well as successful mourning for people with learning disabilities (see Chapter 7 on reminiscence).

Environmental factors

As we have begun to see, when a parent dies, many people with learning disabilities not only have to cope with all the usual difficult feelings that occur at a time of bereavement, but there can be many other factors which could complicate their grieving. Some of these may be located in complex relationships or in developmental understanding, but others may be located in the environment in which the bereaved person is living. For example, in some situations they may not be told of the death straightaway; professional carers or families may feel a need to 'protect' them. They may also not be included in the rituals surrounding the death (Oswin 1982,1991, Deutsch 1985, Kloeppel & Hollins 1989). Being left out will make it more difficult for the person to accept what has happened and to begin to grieve. This exclusion may occur because the carers believe that the learning disabled family member will not understand, or perhaps because of the perception, accurate or otherwise, that it may be impossible for other bereaved members of the family to give the support needed. Whatever the reason, it is likely that this will complicate the grief process for the individual. With forward planning and more knowledge these situations could be prevented. Most research in this field suggests that training for carers, planning ahead and setting up bereavement guidance could help prevent complications develop (Kloeppel & Hollins 1989, Harper & Wadsworth 1993).

If the person with learning disabilities is living in the family home when a parent dies, there may also be multiple losses for that person.

People with learning disabilities often lead very lonely lives, as is explored more fully in later chapters. They are therefore less likely than others to receive informal support when they are bereaved. They may thus come to rely heavily on other surviving members of the family, themselves also experiencing bereavement. All family members will grieve in their own individual way, and sometimes this can be in direct conflict with another family member's grief. I know of one such man with learning disabilities. When his father died, his mother was so overcome with chronic grief that she visited the grave everyday for several years. She wanted her son to accompany her, and this led to arguments and disagreements. The man himself showed few visible signs of grieving the father to whom he had been previously very close; his mother's grief appeared to have inhibited his own. Sometimes simply having friends who are less directly affected by the death that one can talk to can be helpful.

What can be done to make grief less complicated for people with learning disabilities?

What can we do practically to make a difference? Four main points can be drawn from the above:

1 **This chapter has recognised that people with learning disabilities often have little knowledge or experience of death.**
   Groups could be set up to provide education, which could enhance and build upon experiences already gained (see Chapter 8)

2 **Professionals and family carers are often lacking in confidence when it comes to providing support when a person with learning disabilities is bereaved.**
   Training and support regarding bereavement should be provided to professionals and also family carers when appropriate. (see Chapter 10)

3 **Workers involved with people with learning disabilities often overlook the signs of stress, which may be connected to previous losses.**
   This could also be addressed through training, and also through carefully thought-out policies made with bereavement issues in mind (see Chapter 10)

4 People with learning disabilities are often lonely.
Support could be provided to enable them to build friendships and
wider relationships beyond the family, so that they might have a
network of people, comprised of both peers and others, who they can
trust and talk to when they need to (see Chapter 10)

For a variety of reasons, there may be situations when people with
learning disabilities who have been bereaved are not coping even with
good support from staff. If this is the case, a referral to a bereavement
therapist or counsellor would be appropriate (see Chapters 6 & 10).
Services should find out what support is available in the local area before
the need to make a referral arises. There may be psychologists with
relevant counselling skills, or counsellors or creative therapists within the
local learning disability community team. There may also be local
counselling organisations, or bereavement services (such as Cruse
Bereavement Care, a UK based charity offering bereavement counselling), which provide access to people with learning disabilities (see
Resources List). If there is very little precedent in the area for referrals
for clients with learning disabilities, and there appears to be no agency
with the relevant skills and experience, services might think of working in
partnership with the local community team and bereavement service in
order to set up a training day and raise local awareness of this need.

Chapter 4

How grief manifests itself

Recently, as I was posting a card to a friend whose husband had just died, I stopped to think of the many bereaved clients with learning disabilities whom I had seen over the years, and I wondered whether any of them had received messages of condolence after the deaths of their loved ones. In the card to my friend, I acknowledged the sad news and told her that I was thinking of her. I wondered to myself how many of my clients felt that there were people in their lives who really loved and cared about them, and who were 'holding them in mind'.

I thought of another friend, widowed a few years earlier. I pictured her house at the time of her husband's death; full to bursting with cards sending thoughts of love and expressions of how much he would also be missed by others. I know that however hard it was for her and her daughters at that time, one of the things that helped was the visible sign of all the love that surrounded them, and the knowledge that the man they had loved was a special person who had meant a great deal to other people.

And yet, of all the bereaved people with learning disabilities I have met over the years, I have never heard of one of them receiving this sort of concrete response from people around them. If this is the case generally, and I suspect that it all too painfully is, then it is one of many invisible signs of disregard for the grief of people with learning disabilities shown by society.

One of the greatest difficulties for this group of people has been the lack of recognition of their grief. Up until the late 1970s and early 1980s when some pioneering work took place (Emerson 1977, Deutsch 1985, Oswin 1991, see Chapter 2) it was often thought that people with learning disabilities did not form significant attachments to the people in their lives, and would therefore not notice if a particular individual was no longer around. This erroneous belief informed the institutionalisation of large numbers of people into the long stay hospitals. It was also thought that people with learning disabilities would not understand what had happened when someone died (Kitching 1987, Oswin 1991, Conboy-Hill 1992) and therefore that the bereaved person would not grieve.

However, even now with more awareness, it is still easy for people - residential staff, day-centre staff, families and so on not to recognize when someone, especially someone with a learning disability, is grieving. This may be because the person is not expressing themselves in ways that might be expected. People with learning disabilities do not always find it easy to recognize or to express their feelings; although it must be said that at a time of bereavement, it is difficult for most people to communicate to others, regardless of whether they are usually good at communicating or not. There is no right or wrong way of doing this. But difficulties in expression may be compounded by the difficulties others have in understanding or even in listening effectively. Care staff in residential services, for example, are often young and untrained, and may not have experienced bereavement themselves. They may have a stereotyped idea as to how someone should respond and also think that the person should 'be over it' within quite a short time scale. Staff may also feel frightened of openly acknowledging bereavement for fear of the depth of feelings that may be aroused (Kitching 1987); they may feel that they will be unable to offer adequate support, feel unsure about their own feelings about death and be worried as to whether they will cope emotionally themselves.

Working with people who are bereaved requires a great deal of emotional involvement. This is often not encouraged in care settings (Kitching 1987). Care staff receive very little training about anything connected to supporting people's emotional life; training is more focussed on health and safety issues. It would be good to think that with the introduction of the Learning Disability Award Framework as part of the UK Government White Paper *Valuing People* (2002), staff training will become more regulated and things might change for the better (and see Chapter 10). However, it remains to be seen whether this framework will really embrace the importance of enabling residential staff to understand and respond to people's emotional needs. In the meantime, this chapter identifies some of the many different ways in which grief can be overlooked, and at how it can manifest itself when direct expression is difficult.

Unacknowledged grief

Unacknowledged grief, also referred to as disenfranchised grief (Doka 1989), is an emotional burden that can lead to mental ill health (Worden, 1983, Machin 2003). Bereavement is a period during which people are often emotionally vulnerable. Without the support of others, or acknowledgment of the state of mourning, it is more likely that a person will experience a problematic bereavement. Research also identifies possible links between unresolved, repressed or complicated grief, and mental ill health (Zisook & De Vaul 1976, Shorr & Speed 1963).

A number of researchers have claimed that people with learning disabilities manifest the full range of mental health conditions seen in the general population (Sovner and Hurley 1983). However, it has been highlighted that there are enormous problems regarding diagnosis in this population, due to factors such as verbal communication and diagnostic overshadowing (when the learning disability masks the mental health condition). This means that other sources, such as third party reports and observation are heavily relied upon. This therefore points to the importance of staff training, as it is frontline staff and families who are in the best position to detect the early onset of mental distress (See Chapter 10).

In 1977 Patricia Emerson wrote about her experience when working as a consultant to 'emotionally disturbed developmentally disabled clients'. She described how she would often be contacted by different services when a person with a learning disability had suddenly begun to manifest 'emotional and management difficulties', to which they could find no solution. She described the symptoms as including either verbal or physical aggression, or extreme withdrawal. Emerson discovered that in fifty percent of cases there had been either the death or loss of someone close to the client. What is interesting (and indeed horrifying) about her account is that neither the staff within the day-centres or residential services, nor the families, nor even the staff at the crisis intervention centres had thought to link the behaviour with any precipitating factors in the person's life. Emerson describes how traditional mental health settings utilizing crisis intervention methods would routinely try to find a precipitating stress. These same clinics, however, when presented with a client with learning disabilities, often did not ask the same sort of questions that they would of a non-learning disabled client. She underlines the importance of looking carefully at the manner in which the bereavement was handled, once information is available concerning the events surrounding the loss. From her experience a number of circumstances had usually occurred:

1 The staff or family may have denied the event or were unwilling to admit that it had significance
2 The family, staff and peers have given inappropriate emotional responses to the grieving person
3 Family and staff may not have allowed or facilitated an emotional response by the bereaved person
4 Adequate time for an adjustment period to the changes in the client's life had not been allowed
5 The family might have misdirected angry feelings over the death or separation towards the client

Why does this sort of thing happen? Why have crises intervention services not thought to collect bereavement histories from this client group as a matter of course? Is it because of the difficulty gathering a life history from someone who has a learning disability? I suggest this is not the reason, because there is likely to be similar difficulties for psychotic clients, and it is usually possible to gather enough evidence from the people supporting the person and or their family.

So is it just blatant discrimination from all areas of the support network? It would be easy to pass it off as this; but I think that something else is at work on a deeper level. Elsewhere in this book I explore the theory that people who are in supporting roles to people with learning disabilities feel deskilled and inexperienced in knowing what to do or say when one of the people they are supporting becomes bereaved. I think that sometimes it is also too painful to act in a conscious way, when confronted with the double loss of disability and bereavement (and see Chapter 10). Sinason (1992) puts it this way:

> It is bad enough that the normal have to face the sight of the handicapped; to face the extent of grief and depression too is clearly not allowed. The handicapped, like the fat and the old and the ugly, must be funny. (p. 144)

Think of the stereotype of the 'jolly' person with Down syndrome who is 'always' happy. Sinason (1992) describes the phenomenon of the 'handicapped smile', which, in response to society's expectations, many people with learning disabilities employ as a defence mechanism in order to mask emotional pain and to elicit comfortable responses from the people around them. With this in mind, is it any wonder that when we are confronted with someone with a learning disability who is behaving angrily or who is sad, it makes us feel uncomfortable? It does not fit the stereotype. The person may be seen as 'deviant' or 'attention seeking' rather than communicating something painful, and their grief is ignored or forgotten.

It is important to realize the full implication of this sort of blindness, as it is lack of support and total misreading of the situation that could contribute to more complex grieving. This may be the reason why people are often left out of funeral arrangements or are expected to carry on with their daily routine of day-care or college without any consideration given to the possible need for 'compassionate leave', which the rest of us might expect from our own working environments. Worden (1983) states the importance of inclusion in rituals and good support during a time of bereavement as factors which can help to determine a healthy grieving process. It is therefore essential that basic training in understanding bereavement is provided for direct care staff as a preventative measure (see Chapter 10).

How might we know if someone with a learning disability is grieving?

Given that we have just seen how the bereavement of people with learning disabilities is often not acknowledged or, if it is, that the person is expected not to be affected by it and to carry on as usual, we can expect that information about this kind of major life circumstance may well not get communicated to the various social and support networks around the person. The person themselves may find it hard to communicate what has happened clearly, as discussed above. It often becomes a matter of guesswork, if not detective work, for those who are supporting people with learning disabilities to discover what it is that may be affecting the person, and causing them to act differently to the way that is usual for them. The likelihood is that if someone is feeling distressed and they cannot tell the people around them, they will show it another way, usually through their behaviour. It has been noted that aggressive behaviour may be the only way for some people with profound learning disabilities to express their upset and confusion when they are bereaved (McLoughlin 1986).

In one of the first papers written about the reaction of learning disabled children to bereavement (Ray 1977), the reaction of two boys to the death of their fathers is described. Each found it difficult to grasp the concept, but were none the less very distressed by the absence of their fathers. For one of the boys, this was made even more confusing because his mother did not know how to explain that he had died, and instead told her son that his father was at work. Each of the boys displayed searching behaviour, and one also tried to self-harm. Sometimes reactions can be more introverted; the person may show signs of depression such as lack of appetite, becoming listless and neglecting personal care. But what is clear is that limited comprehension of the death concept does not protect someone from the painful reactions to bereavement (Cathcart 1995).

In 1997, Hollins and Esterhuyzen studied the reactions of people with learning disabilities to bereavement. They compared fifty parent-bereaved people with learning disabilities and fifty non-bereaved people with learning disabilities. The result showed that aberrant behaviours are more frequent among the group who had been bereaved. There were significantly more cases of what they termed 'psychopathological morbidity' in this group. They also found, as had Emerson (1977), that staff did not usually attribute behavioural problems to the bereavement and its consequent life changes, nor was there a recognition of psychopathology due to bereavement.

Oswin (1984) studied the effect of the short-term loss of a parent on disabled children in respite care. She charted the children's grief caused by the experience of short term care; this was expressed in specific patterns of behaviour. I have also observed similar sorts of behaviour in adults with learning disabilities who have been bereaved. She described one pattern as 'searching'. Here she noted that the children posted themselves very close to a door or window, and paced, seeming unable to concentrate on anything, as though they were waiting for the parent to return. Oswin described a second behaviour as 'bewilderment', when the child wandered aimlessly or rummaged in cupboards or toy boxes unable to focus on the objects, as though they were looking for something that was not there. 'Clinging' occurred when a child selected a carer to attach themselves to, and would not let them out of their sight; they often tried to sit on their lap when they sat down, and attempted to follow them every-where they went. Reassurance-seeking behaviour was seen in children repeatedly asking anxious questions such as "Mummy come?". 'Protest' was how Oswin labelled the angry behaviour which she often noted happening around meal times, the child frequently manufacturing an angry situation by, picking on another child for example, or throwing a cup. 'Withdrawal' was the opposite; here the child refused to eat, or spent their time curled up in a ball, not wanting to join in anything. Oswin also described very regressed behaviour where the child seemed to have lost skills that they used to have, such as continence or literacy, or perhaps eating solids or being able to use a knife and fork.

Strachan (1981) found many similar responses amongst the bereaved residents of a large institution. He described how one man became agitated and uncooperative, and how another became irritable and unchar-acteristically incontinent. Kitching (1987) also describes uncharacteristic episodes of aggression. It is important to recognize that some of these things are a normal part of mourning, but when they seem to be going on for a long time and there are relatively few 'good days', then there is cause for concern. Many of these observations have similarities to those made by the Robertsons (1953) when they observed children who had been separated from their mothers in early infancy. These findings informed the attachment theories of Bowlby (1973) (see Chapter 3).

Response to loss through behaviour

The way that we form our early attachment with our primary carer will inform the relationships that we consequently make and break throughout our life. It is therefore important to consider supporting a person and trying to better understand the expression of their grief in the light of that person's early attachment experience.

New research carried out by Parkes (in press, personal communication 2003) confirms that insecure attachments between parents and children contribute to complications with bereavement. This is an important piece of research to consider when trying to understand the effects of bereave-ment on people with learning disabilities, as many children born with a learning disability are likely to experience complex attachment. Parkes' research involved one hundred and eighty one people who had been referred for psychiatric help after bereavement. The subjects were asked to complete questionnaires which focused on their early attachment experience. He found there to be a link between insecure attachments and difficulties with current methods of coping with distress. This suggests that problematic parenting predisposes people to difficulty in expressing emotions and in trusting people, and when under stress, they may turn in on themselves or distress may be expressed in hidden ways.

Parkes attempted to ascertain the links between particular types of attachment and how these in turn affected grief responses. His findings have confirmed that people who had secure attachments tended to make secure attachments in later life, and were less extremely affected by bereavement. Parkes also found that people who had Anxious /Ambivalent attachments, (those who had anxious parents, who would have given their child the impression that they would not survive unless they stayed close to them) were prone to clinging, and to severe and protracted grief; these people would have grown up with low self-trust and their trust in others may be excessive.

Parkes had expected that people who had parents who were intolerant of closeness and therefore had developed an Avoidant attachment might experience delayed grief, but instead found that delayed grief seemed to mostly follow traumatic bereavements and was less to do with attachment patterns (although he does suggest that the numbers involved may be too small to be significant regarding this finding). However, he did note that this group tended to grow up finding it hard to trust others, and had difficulty in expressing affection or grief in adult life. They may also have a tendency to show less empathy for others and to be more aggressive to their peers. Finally, people who had Disorganised/Disorientated Attachments (these people are likely to have experienced abuse and neglect) were seen to have a tendency to grow up lacking trust in themselves and others; they may often show 'learned helplessness' and a tendency to self harm. These factors suggest that they may be prone to anxiety, depression and high alcohol consumption following bereavement. At a time of separation, all of these patterns of behaviour (informed by early attachment) are likely to show more strongly, because the person's security has been undermined.

With disrupted attachments in mind, I would like to consider two different services for people with learning disabilities. Firstly, an assessment and treatment service; a residential service to which people with learning disabilities are referred when they are at a point of crisis. It is often the case that their present residential situation has broken down. For example, the individual's behaviour may have become too challenging for their current residential home or family home to manage, or they may be showing signs of mental distress, such as self-harm.

The second service is a medium secure unit for people with learning disabilities who have committed a criminal offence. The residents of this unit will have gone through judicial procedures before finally ending up there. Although these two services are different there is a similarity, in that people referred to them have pushed the boundaries to an extreme and it is their behaviour which has become the cause for concern.

In my clinical work with residents in an assessment and treatment unit, it is clear that loss of various sorts features very strongly in all of these people's lives. I see their behaviour as being a consequence of this in many situations. A high percentage of the women who come into the service, for example, have had babies, which they have subsequently had to give up. There are many people whose parents have died, and there are also many families where parents have separated.

As a consequence of my involvement in this service, I have brought the issue of loss to the attention of the unit management; in response, I have been supported, along with a colleague, to develop a Loss and Bereavement training programme for all staff working in the unit (approximately one hundred). This is delivered in groups of about ten, each training consisting of five two-hour sessions. We have also developed a Loss and Bereavement policy for the service that includes among other things, the gathering of a loss history for all residents on admission. When the training is completed, we will be offering a regular supervision group, for staff who are supporting a resident experiencing difficulty coping with a loss. The aim of this programme of work with the staff is to raise awareness amongst the team of the impact of loss and its expression amongst the client group. It also to strengthen the confidence of the staff team in working positively and supportively with this issue.

My work in the assessment and treatment service has led me to enquire about the issue of loss for residents in other specialised units, where people with learning disabilities have been admitted due to extreme difficulties with managing their behaviour. This has included medium secure units. I carried out some initial research into the loss history of residents in one of these medium secure units, and discovered that every one of the people detained there had experienced a significant loss, many of which had occurred in childhood. A quick review of the patients who had been admitted to the unit revealed that several of the detainees had experienced the death of a parent, some at an early age. Many had experienced their parents' separation, many, again, at an early age. For some individuals, the early death of the parent resulted in the child being moved from the family home into a children's home. At least one person had been removed from the family home before their first year. Only two out of thirty people still had both parents living together.

It would appear that the majority of the detainees had experienced very disrupted childhoods, which might include changes of carers, loss of carers and death of carers, as well as physical and sexual abuse. This is a broad picture of loss, but one that indicates that this is an area highly worthy of further research. It would be pertinent to ascertain whether their loss has been acknowledged or recognized, or not, whether they had made firm attachments in the early years, or whether there had been difficulties from birth.

Clearly, not all people with learning disabilities who have experienced insecure attachments will end up within these kinds of services. But for those who have, or who may, future research which considered what factors might contribute to this outcome would be of value. Services acquiring a greater understanding of what elements are likely to lead to residential placements breaking down, or to criminal behaviour, would be of enormous benefit to people with learning disabilities in particular, and to wider society in general.

Chapter 5

Compounded losses

When a person with a learning disability experiences the death of a parent, they often experience many other losses and major life changes at the same time. The first part of this chapter examines some of the additional and often unrecognized losses that may occur when a parent dies. It is important to remember that an experience of profound loss may also re-awaken painful feelings from other past losses; this is even more pertinent where there has been no opportunity to work through the feelings from the original loss. This process can contribute to additional complications in the grieving of the current loss. The second part of the chapter will thus examine other major losses that are common in the lives of people with a learning disability, which may lead to compounded grief.

Moving from the family home

A significant proportion of the population of people with learning disabilities are living with members of their family (Walker and Walker 1998, Ward 1998, Department of Health 2001b). It is estimated that forty percent of this population live with elderly parents, and ten percent live with a sole family carer over the age of seventy (Watson and Harker 1993). If a person with a learning disability is living in the family home when a parent dies, this can precipitate a move into residential care. If the deceased was the last remaining parent, the bereaved person may have to move suddenly (Oswin 1989 & 1991) into an unknown setting. Even if there is still one remaining parent, it can often become much more difficult for the surviving parent to manage caring for the person with learning disabilities on their own, particularly if the parent is elderly. It may be that the family coping mechanism is now so out of balance that the perception of the family (and possibly that of supporting services) is that the family can no longer continue caring for the person with learning disabilities at home in the way that they previously did (Worden 1983).

This perception may arise because of the role that the deceased took in the family; they may have been the main carer, the disciplinarian, or the one who had the physical strength to perform certain caring tasks. It might also be because, in reality, both parents were struggling to cope as they became older and more frail; with only one parent surviving, the situation has become impossible. There is often limited support from family or formal services, and informal support networks (such as those built up around organisations such as Mencap) can become vulnerable as the people forming these networks age and need help themselves (Thompson, D. 2002).

The initial move is likely to be to a crisis placement, and there will probably have been no chance for any preparation. This can easily become a permanent move from the long-term family home, with possibly several further moves until a permanent placement is found. The residential placement may not be geographically well situated in terms of familiarity, which will exacerbate the isolation of the person, possibly making it difficult for them to visit family and friends and for people to visit them. If they have moved a long way away from the surviving parent, they may in effect 'lose' both parents at the same time.

The relationship between someone with learning disabilities and their ageing parent is often an interdependent one. This interdependence can exist at several levels; emotional, practical and/or financial (Thompson, D 2002, Magrill et al 1997). The person with learning disabilities may have been the sole carer for a frail elderly parent (Walker et al, 1996; Magrill et al 1997), carrying out important tasks such as shopping, cleaning and cooking. This role may have been almost invisible to anyone outside the immediate family unit, overlooked because society so often has very limited expectations of people with learning disabilities. Yet the person may have carried out a vital role, in making it possible for themselves and their parent to continue to live independently in their own home. When the person is then bereaved and leaves the family home, they may be placed in residential care, which offers high support. This may leave the person feeling deskilled and purposeless. This is a particular danger when someone is assessed for a new home shortly after bereavement when they may well not be functioning at their best (Oswin 1985, 1991).

Bereavement literature warns against making major life changes or decisions during the first year of bereavement (Parkes 1972). It is recognized that when someone is bereaved, their state of mind may be too unstable to make clear decisions. There are already many changes arising from the death to which the bereaved person needs to become accustomed. It is usually better, therefore, to make decisions once the other changes have been lived with for a while. Yet many people with learning disabilities find themselves in the sort of situations described above, and have had no part in the decisions made on their behalf, and no preparation for yet another major life change. They are, in effect, having to cope with multiple losses; the loss of people who are important to them, their home, familiarity of routine, familiar environment, a sense of competence through using skills, a meaningful role, and informal contact with family and friends.

They also have to cope with adjusting to new people and new ways of doing things (Oswin 1989). For someone for whom communication is difficult, this may be the first time they have had to live without the people around them who understand them best. All of this in addition to grieving the dead loved one, itself a difficult task for people who may already be finding it difficult to understand the full extent of what has happened. In many ways, their situation resembles that of refugees, suddenly transplanted after trauma into an alien culture and language, far away from everything familiar and precious.

The reality may be that taking into account the situations in which many bereaved people with learning disabilities find themselves, individuals show remarkable resilience and resourcefulness. Oswin's (1989) description of 'Jane' who was bereaved of both her parents within a few years of each other, demonstrates the importance of the circumstances surrounding someone who is mourning, how these affect the way in which the person grieves, and sometimes, the rest of their life. I would like to reflect on this woman's story, and look closely at some of the elements that affected the outcome of both bereavements.

Jane's experience of the death of each of her parents could not have been more different. When her father died she had the support of her friends, her mother and the day service. She had seen her father's health deteriorate, so she was, to some extent, prepared for his death. She saw him in his coffin and she took part in the funeral; her mother spoke to her about her father's death using a religious framework that was meaningful to them both. Jane also had a useful role in looking after her mother, and they shared their grief. Everyone in her support network was aware of her situation, and this was reflected in the way they behaved towards her. At her day-centre, she made a vase in pottery, to take to her father's grave, and in her drama group, they acted out scenes of funerals. The staff supported her to communicate about her father using her own sign language, which had evolved over a number of years at home with her parents. Jane had days when she was very sad, but this eased over time.

When her mother dies very suddenly a few years later, having just seen her daughter off on the bus to the day-centre, Jane never returns home again. Staff at the day-centre break the news to her, and her social worker goes to the family house to collect some clothes. She does not take Jane because she fears that it will upset her. A distant family member organizes the funeral, and Jane is not invited. She is moved to a long stay hospital twenty miles away. The hospital staff are not interested in hearing about the sign language that Jane has used at home, and state that they will teach her makaton (a recognised sign language taught to people with learning disabilities and the staff working with them). Staff from the day-centre are discouraged from visiting her as it is believed that they will 'rake up the past', and the hospital staff think that this will upset her. She changes from being a happy, secure woman to one who is described in the ward notes as anxious, aggressive and quarrelsome, eventually becoming withdrawn and passive in her behaviour.

It is not Jane's learning disability that has led to difficulties in adjusting to the death of her mother, but the incredible lack of sensitivity in the system around her. In the crisis, Jane's relocation seems to have taken precedence over everything. It seems to have been forgotten that at the heart of this situation is a woman who has just been bereaved. Jane is given no opportunity to come to terms with what has happened by visiting the family house or by attending the funeral. She is placed in an unfamiliar environment with no access to people she knows. No one takes the time to learn her particular way of communicating. What is disturbing is that in a situation like this, professionals focus on the practical issues such as re-housing and settling someone into a new routine, rather than attending to the person's emotional needs.

(Description of Jane's experiences drawn from Oswin, 1989, with kind permission of the King's Fund, London 2003)

This is a demonstration of how the double taboo of death and disability affects our society; both these elements 'elicit fear and avoidance' (Kloeppel & Hollins 1989). Dealing only with the practicalities may feel more manageable to professionals in the short term, but it can only lead to long term complications for the person themselves. It is the system that cannot accommodate grief, not the person with the learning disability.

Sadly, Jane's story is still far from unusual, even though Oswin was writing more than a decade ago. In light of this, it could be said that we do not acknowledge nearly often enough how well people cope with some of the impossible demands made on them. But what is also clear is that the stress that people experience often goes unnoticed, especially when it is manifested by withdrawal. It is more likely to receive some attention if it is expressed through anger, but then this is often not attributed to loss either (see Chapter 4). As Oswin (1989) remarks,

> ....as customs change and studies of human behaviour offer even more sophisticated explanations of our likely reactions to stress, perhaps the one factor about death that remains constant is the need for those who mourn to receive consideration
>
> (p. 93)

How well do we as a society offer consideration to people with learning disabilities who need to grieve?

> Denying people with mental handicaps their grief, and hiding from them the truth about death, shows a flagrant disregard for their feelings and contributes to the process of dehumanisation. This is made all the more poignant by the move towards advocating their rights in other areas.　　(Kitching 1987, p. 62)

The relationship between an adult with learning disabilities and their parents

In order to understand some of the subtleties of the losses experienced, it is also important to consider the nature of the relationship an adult with learning disabilities might have with their parents.

In his book *Children and Grief* (Guilford 1996),William Worden states that the death of a parent is one of the most fundamental losses a child can face. For people with learning disabilities, this sentiment can continue into adult life, because many people remain dependent on their parents into their adult years. He goes on to say that parents are 'in effect their (children's) partners in negotiating the essential developmental tasks that will take them to adulthood' (p. 9). This is an ideal scenario. The reality is, of course, that parents vary enormously in the extent to which they may fulfill this sort of role. For a child with a learning disability, who has a positive relationship with his or her parents, the role of negotiator is an ongoing task, not just until adulthood but throughout life. The parents may also become mediators for their child/adult offspring, enabling them to interpret the world around them, and helping others to understand their child's needs (even when they become adult).

However, the relationship between parent and disabled child may also be full of complex power struggles. The parent may control rather than empower their offspring; this may come about through difficulties with standing back and allowing the child to take risks, or finding it hard to let their child fail on the path to learning something new. Parents may also feel compelled to 'protect' their child from the critical gaze of society, not wishing them to experience ridicule or rejection. Unfortunately, this is so often the harsh and very painful reality people with learning disabilities and their families have to contend with every day. In order to do this, parents may feel the need to impose strict limits, and to keep a tight reign. There can be complex tensions in any parental relationship between love and hate, but this may be all the more heightened in the relationship between a disabled child and their parents. All of these factors will contribute to a complex power struggle within the relationship.

In my relationship with my own fourteen-year-old daughter, there are regular occasions when she wants to argue or be angry with me, often over very small things. I know that this is something that she needs to do as a natural part of her development, and something which I need to show her I can withstand without it affecting my love for her. Of course she needs to separate emotionally from me, to assert herself and to oppose me sometimes. It is not easy for either of us; but how much harder it would be if she had other needs that kept her also needing to be dependent on me. She might fear my withdrawal, and I might fear for her safety in asserting her independence.

A disabled child is caught between needing to be dependent and yearning for independence. Fears, originating from the parent, of situations perceived as threatening, can become inflated for both parent and child, leading to them becoming caught up in a web of cosy domestic bliss, rarely venturing into the big wide world outside. This in turn further disables the adult child, as his or her experiences of life remain limited. The person with a learning disability may silently comply with this further disabling environment, smile and seem quite happy in the infantalised world because it is safe and because they enjoy the complete attention of the parents. But there may also be a hidden fear of upsetting the person they are most dependent upon.

This of course may be a very real fear, grounded in the unspoken disappointment experienced by the parents at the time of the birth of their disabled child. Ghost of these feelings may always overshadow the relationship. Sometimes this disappointment may be more than a shadow; it may be acted upon. Strickler (2001) reports that people with learning disabilities are at a greater risk than the normal population of being the victims of child abuse, domestic violence and sexual abuse. There can be several contributing factors to this. It may be in part attributed to the fact that children with learning disabilities tend to lack the specific behaviours that non-learning disabled children use to attract attention from their parents. As a result of this, they are less likely to bond with their parents and are more likely to be abused (Valentine 1990). It can also be because these children place more financial and caretaking demands on the family, which in turn contributes to the stress load on the parent (op cit.), and this can be exacerbated by parental isolation. The parent may also place unrealistic expectations on the child, which the child consistently fails to meet.

One of the hardest things for any of the bereaved people with learning disabilities that I have supported has been to express or acknowledge that there was ever any anger in the relationship with their parents. And yet, time and again, within a short period in most situations, there is evidence of anger towards the parent. Not just the usual grief-anger of abandonment, but rage that has never dared to show itself. This can range from blame for the disability itself, to anger about imposed limitations, or for being abandoned in hospital or boarding school, for being made to feel stupid, clumsy or in the way, or for receiving unbelievable cruelty from family members.

One lady reminisced about her mother's cooking. She remembered her mother's Sunday roasts: *"I was not allowed to help, I was always in the way"*. When I asked a little more, this lady told me that she had longed to help; she knew that she would have been able to peel the potatoes or make the mint sauce, but she had had to remain passive and not "get in the way". She had a very close and loving relationship with her mother, but there was no room in it for anger. She feared that she would have lost her mother's love if she had argued with her or challenged her in any way.

In my experience, when anger of this kind is acknowledged, there can be overwhelming pain felt for the loss of *what might have been*. It was Freud who first wrote of the internal conflict that all humans have between love and hate. Inner conflict is a necessary and a healthy state to be in, so long as the important other people in one's life have the capacity to withstand some anger. However, when we experience conflict such as anger and hate towards someone whom we also love, it raises our anxiety and we may feel guilty. It is our ability to manage these conflicting feelings that is the key to our mental well-being.

People with learning disabilities who have been treated with violence, or sexually abused by a parent, frequently have very low self-esteem; their concentration can be poor, and they may have difficulty in initiating or maintaining social contact. In one group, Laura, a woman in her fifties, told group members how her father had regularly hit her with his belt, as had other men within the family. Understandably, this became something that Laura needed to repeat to the group in answer to everything else that was being spoken about. It was as though she felt that she would never be heard, as indeed she had not been for many years.

Loss of a parent, therefore, although of huge significance for nearly everyone when it occurs, can be a particularly complex loss for someone with a learning disability, for the losses bound up within that relationship may be many and complicated. Sometimes the lack of a positive relationship with parents even before their death can be experienced as a loss, especially when there is also an abusive or neglectful element. This can throw a shadow over the way that a person lives their life.

Julie is a woman in her forties, described as having a mild learning disability and obsessive compulsive disorder. She lived in a long stay hospital from early childhood until her twenties when she moved into a hostel. She left the hostel in her thirties to live independently, which she managed for ten years. Her siblings and her elderly parents are still alive; although she has some contact with them, the relationships can be ambivalent and difficult. Julie experienced a traumatic incident in early childhood, when she was living at home with her family; she fell into an open fire and suffered extensive burns, and still feels great discomfort from the scars which resulted from the accident. She is on antidepressants that have been prescribed to treat her obsessional behaviour.

Julie had held down a catering job for about twenty years; when I first met her, she had been referred to the service because of the loss she was experiencing having been made redundant. One of her other major difficulties at the time of referral was the exploitative relationships which she had become caught up in. Her 'friends' would often call round to her flat and ask to 'borrow' money which they never repaid. They often seemed to come on the day that she took out her benefit, and she felt powerless to keep them out of her flat or to say no to them. She had also recently reported that one of the men from this group had seriously sexually assaulted her. It is a common response amongst people who have been subjected to abusive behaviour in a domestic setting to display compliance, which contributes to an increased sense of helplessness and vulnerability (Murphy and Razza 1998).

The loss of the job had come as a serious blow to Julie; her self-esteem, which was low anyway, took a nosedive. Julie had now lost her sense of routine and purpose. She has a tendency to worry obsessively about things and can show obsessive behaviour, both these traits frequently worsening when she has time on her hands. One of the obsessive behaviours that Julie adopts at times of stress is talking to electric sockets. She carries one around in her handbag in order that she can talk to it whenever she feels the need. The redundancy seemed to have awakened many other losses for her, and connected her back to other times of rejection and feeling unwanted.

When Julie entered my consulting room for the first session, she was accompanied by her social worker, who she wanted to remain in the room with her for a while. It is important to mention here that my room is situated within the grounds of a long stay hospital that was at this time in the process of being closed down; the buildings will continue to be used to house specialist community services such as mine. As Julie walked through the room and before she had even reached her seat, she began talking to the electric sockets in the room. She told them to behave; I wondered whether she was warning herself or me to behave. She was very curious about the hospital and wondered if she could come and stay in it for a bit. I thought that perhaps she was feeling unsafe where she was living now, and wondered whether Julia thought that if she were back in hospital, people would be able to look after her.

In the second session she came with two different escorts, and she wanted both of them to stay in the room with her for the entire session. She told me about her friend Monica, who had been round to her flat and asked for forty pounds which Julie had given to her. She asked me if I thought Monica might be dead. I said that I wondered if perhaps sometimes she felt so angry with Monica that she wished she would die, and that she was worried that by having these thoughts, she might have killed her. At the third session, Julie chose to come into my room on her own for the first time, and the first thing she said was that Monica was not dead. She told me that again Monica had been to visit and asked for money, which she had given her. This time I wondered if she felt that she had to give Monica the money because that act of giving would counteract the possibility of her angry thoughts killing Monica off. Julie smiled when I said this; something in what I said seemed to ring true for her.

In the next session, I asked Julie about the scar on her neck, and she told me how she had fallen into the fire when she was a baby. She said, "I could have died. My Mum doesn't care, nor does my Dad". I asked her if she could tell me when in her life someone had cared for her, or had been able to look after her. She remembered one particular nurse from when she lived in the long stay hospital, whom she felt had really cared for her; but she said that it was a long time ago, and she no longer knew where the nurse was. I said it was hard to take care of yourself if nobody cared for you. She replied, "I can't come and live here because it's closing, isn't it?" I told her that was true, but affirmed that being cared for was what she seemed to want at that moment. We talked about her job; she described what she did when she was working, and said that she really missed it. She felt that the people she worked with cared about her and that they would notice that she wasn't there any more. She told me that she lay in bed until late now, as there seemed no point in getting up. As we finished the session I was left with the impression of a very young neglected child, and felt that Julie had been very much in touch with that part of herself that day.

In the next session, however, I noted a difference in the way in which Julie greeted the socket as she came into the room; she said a very friendly 'hello' to it, in a funny chirpy sort of voice. I felt that this was her way of saying hello to me; it seemed to say that she now felt comfortable coming to see me and that she was beginning to trust me. She spoke about her skin graft hurting, and that her skin felt tight; I suggested that perhaps she was also telling me that she was hurting in other ways. She told me that her Mum should have gone to prison, because she had pushed her in the fire. Then almost as quickly, she changed the story and said that her Mum had been in the kitchen and that she had been on her own in the living room with the fire and had fallen in. Perhaps she was protecting her Mum by telling the second version and also herself from the painfulness of that story, or perhaps she wasn't sure of the truth and lived with both versions in her head. Either way, she was left with the reality of a dangerous murderous mother or a neglectful disinterested mother. Both versions of this truth affected the way Julie lived her life now; she was left feeling unlovable and worthless. This is perhaps why people could just walk into her flat and take her money and abuse her body; she did not feel she had any right to stop them.

We were coming up to a summer break. Several times in this session, Julie had asked how many times we would meet until the break and she checked several times if I would still be here the following week, (or would I be a neglectful mother and forget her?). She then said it would be Christmas soon (she knew that at Christmas, the hospital would be closing and the last few remaining residents would be moving out, and possibly some of the buildings would be demolished). She then said, "The sockets will go when they pull the hospital down, won't they?". I asked her what she felt about Christmas; she replied that she didn't like it and she asked me if I had a Mum and Dad. I thought that she was thinking about her own family. She wanted to draw a picture; she chose very bright coloured pastels - orange, yellow and green. She drew a house with yellow windows and a large bright sun. She said it was her Mum's house. I said that maybe she would like to have a good relationship with her Mum; she looked sad and said yes.

After the summer break Julie asked about the hospital being demolished, and wondered whether our room would also be pulled down (at that time I was not sure, but I was able to reassure her that I would always have a room to see her in). She wondered again what would happen to the sockets. She told me that sometimes the sockets were friendly and that sometimes they weren't. She said that they didn't care when she fell in the fire. She said that her Mum didn't want her, which was why she went to live in the hospital, and that she used to dress the babies when she lived there. She said she didn't want to come and live here anymore. She wondered whether the sockets would be here after Christmas, to which I replied that perhaps she was wondering whether I would still be here after Christmas. Strangely at this point, I was suddenly very aware of feeling overwhelmingly tired, and it was just then that Julie asked what we would do if there was a fire. I said we would have to go together and stand out on the grass where it was safe, and that I felt that she was checking with me to see if I could take care of her, whether she was safe with me. At the end of the session she said that it had gone very quickly.

During this time in her life outside the sessions, Julie had been able to stand up to the people who had been bullying her and they no longer came round, but she still felt very vulnerable. Her social worker had sought a more sheltered placement for her, where she would still have independence but there would also be staff that she could ask for support if she needed it. At this point she was preparing to move. She was feeling concerned because she had understood that she would only be able to stay in her new flat for five years (which was not the reality). My sense was that she felt that no-one would be able to bear her for very long, so she was already preparing herself for rejection. She said that she didn't want to find herself back on her own; she wanted to build up new friendships. She had seen that they were building new bungalows on the hospital site and she said she wanted to move into one of them so that she could be near me. Again in this session I was aware of overwhelming sleepiness, which was a new experience for me. I have come to think of it as my counter transference response to the unbearable well of loneliness and rejection that Julie feels.

The following week Julie arrived ten minutes early, and I asked her to wait outside. When she came in to the room, she told the sockets off. I said that I thought that she was cross with me. She replied, "I'm not cross with you, it's the sockets". It seemed safer to project her anger onto inanimate objects such as the sockets, than to express them directly to me. The following week she said she was hungry when she came in and she asked me how the sockets were. We talked about the sockets, and she described them as her friends; she missed the ones in the hospital where she had lived. She said they never spoke to her, they just listened, and that she carried one around in her bag so that she could talk to it. Julie told me that she talked to her socket less now that she talked to me, and to other people. She said she felt worried for the people moving out of the hospital where I worked, because it reminded her of how anxious she had felt when she was moving from the hospital where she had lived. She said that she would like to live in the hospital, because then she could see me more often.

At the beginning of one session Julie burst in through the door and told me that she had had an accident on the bus the day before and been injured. She said that she could have been killed, she couldn't breathe, and she could have collapsed. She didn't go to hospital because she didn't know how to get there, so she went into a café to recover, and said that people had stared at her. She said to the socket "how would you like it, you haven't been in an accident". From the questions that I asked her about this incident, I gathered that it was not a very serious accident and that she was probably not really in any great danger. The point was she perceived herself to be.

Research (e.g. Brownell and Congress 1998) shows somatic complaints have been found in women who have been victims of domestic abuse, and in survivors of traumatic incidents. Such complaints include trauma responses such as jumpiness and hypervigilance and anxiety reactions such as trembling and heart palpitations, which Julie clearly experienced at this time. She unconsciously made the link herself as during the same session she referred back to the time of the fire. She said that the first socket that she remembered was in the local general hospital when she was there recovering from the fire; then she linked back to the recent accident and said that her socket could have got broken, that she could have died. She remembered being on a drip after the fire, and having a blood transfusion. She remembered that there was a socket just behind her bed that "cheered her up, when she was stuck in bed on the drip and lonely". She said that other patients didn't talk to her and her family didn't visit very often, so she talked to the socket.

She came into a session telling me that one of the men who had bullied and raped her when she was living in her previous flat had recently been the victim of theft; some boys had run off with his wallet. Then she told the socket off for laughing. I suggested that she felt like laughing because it had been him and not her who this had happened to; perhaps she felt that he deserved it. The socket seemed to serve several purposes for her; she could use it as a container in which to project 'dangerous feelings and thoughts', she could use it as a confidante, and sometimes it almost seemed to be a part of her, as in "it could have been broken in the accident, I could have been killed".

There is a very real danger when working with people with learning disabilities that behavioural and psychological responses to early abuse are not recognised or are misdiagnosed (Craine et al 1988). Once Julie's behaviour was recognised for the coping mechanism that it was, it could be talked about and reflected on with her, which in turn led to her becoming less dependent on it, and also to her appearing less eccentric. This made it easier for her to fit in socially, and to make friends.

Unacknowledged loss connected to sexuality

For many people with learning disabilities, emotional and physical intimacy are major factors missing from their lives altogether or are perhaps carried out as covert activities. All around them they see people in relationships, their parents, adult siblings, staff and so on, and this is reinforced by images in newspapers and on television.

Historically the sexuality of people with learning disabilities has been both denied and feared (Craft and Craft 1979, McCarthy 1999). There are two opposing ways of thinking behind these two attitudes. The first stems from the belief that people with learning disabilities are 'eternal children', which leads to them being treated as such for the whole of their lives (Kempton 1972, Craft & Craft 1983, McCarthy 1999). Some parents of people with learning disabilities find it difficult to accept the inevitable dawning of sexuality as their child grows up. They have perhaps grown to accept having a child with a disability, but cannot cope with the idea of this child growing up and all the complications that come with maturation. When this situation occurs, the person's sexuality can become denied, and they become thought of as asexual. Research has demonstrated   that children with disabilities have the same emotional and sexual drives as other children, but are given less knowledge (Gordon 1972); yet in order to comply, the person themselves may split off any sexual knowledge or feelings (Sinason 1992):

> ...any signs of sexual interest or arousal were ignored, repressed or misunderstood. In addition...it was thought essential to keep them in a state of ignorance about sex
>
> (McCarthy 1999, p. 53)

In direct contrast, the other view as described by Mc Carthy (1999) is of 'people with learning disabilities as being potentially dangerous. This was based on the idea that they were unable to control themselves...' (p. 53). She continues:

> ...it was thought that people with learning disabilities would have an uncontrolled sexuality, that they would be 'over-sexed', sexually promiscuous. In short, they were thought to be a potential sexual threat to others.   (op.cit)

Another belief system that has informed the treatment of people with learning disabilities stems from the eugenics theories that have been described elsewhere in this book. This belief feared that disadvantaged and immoral members of society would erode the heritage of the nation. Society has historically found various ways of restricting people with learning disabilities from having sexual relationships. One action taken with this fear in mind was the incarceration of people with learning disabilities in large institutions. Inside the institutions, men and women were kept segregated. Another way of managing this fear was through mass sterilisation, although this was far more prevalent in the USA than in Britain. However as recently as 1994, China introduced its own eugenics laws to reduce the number of 'inferior births'; amongst other things this law allows the state to prevent people with disabilities from marrying or having children (Fletcher 2001).

We have witnessed the effect of another important philosophy over the last two decades, that of 'normalisation'. This is a concept that originates from Denmark and spread to the whole of Scandinavia in the late 1960s and early 1970s (Bank-Mikkelson 1980, Nirje 1980). The ideas were expanded upon in North America (Wolfensberger 1972, 1983) and eventually came to Britain in the 1980s. This informed the move from long stay institutions into smaller homes in the community. Almost every service for people with learning disabilities in the UK now runs along these principles. With these changes, one might have expected a move towards supporting people with learning disabilities to have more 'normal' emotional and sexual relationships. However, although this may have been the original expectation behind the philosophy, it has not necessarily yet become the reality. Indeed, McCarthy (1999) states that for women, there is little difference in the experiences of those who had lived in hospitals and those living in community settings. She reports that women in both settings are likely to experience sex as an aggressive, often abusive act, and that the majority have little control in deciding 'what they wanted to do, with whom, when and how' (p. 13).

For professionals, the sexuality of clients is still an uncomfortable and taboo area; many residential homes do not accommodate sexual relationships openly. McCarthy (1999) reports that even when a residential service is open to the people with learning disabilities who lived there using their own room for sexual activity, staff were not always good at making this clear to the residents. This was illustrated by the account of two women who lived in the same house; one of the women didn't believe that she would be allowed to bring her boyfriend back to her bedroom, whereas another woman in the same house had the confident view that her bedroom was her own private place where she could lock the door and they would not be disturbed. This perhaps illustrates services' discomfort with the whole area of sexuality; it cannot be and often is not spoken of openly. This can lead to couples feeling that they have nowhere in which to develop loving mutual relationships.

A Swedish physically disabled writer named Enby, quoted by Craft and Craft (1979), gives us an insight into what it must be like to have so little privacy:

> One of the worst features of this is that there is nowhere for the patient to go with her or his friend. It is humiliating to have to hide in cupboards or crawl into culverts like dying elephants - embarrassing to have to ask friends to stand and watch by the door as if one were committing a burglary. There are no rooms for lovers to be in.
>
> (pp. 12-13)

McCarthy asked the women with learning disabilities involved in her research who they could talk to about sex. She discovered that although in theory staff were available to discuss personal matters, in reality this was not the case:

> ...when staff did listen, their responses were sometimes simplistic and unhelpful - for example, to tell the women 'not to do it' or 'that I shouldn't go with men'. Also, two women

were acutely aware of the power staff had, either to get
information about their sexual lives or with regard to what they
might do with it.   (p.134)

Same sex relationships between people with learning disabilities have
historically been '..either ignored, marginalized or pathologised'
(McCarthy 1999, p. 64); however this is beginning to change. Although
very focussed on heterosexual relationships, there was a developing interest in the 1980s in supporting the sexuality of people with learning
disabilities (Craft 1980: Kempton 1988). As the work expanded into the
1990s, there was some movement towards recognising and accepting
same sex relationships. McCarthy (1999) suggests that this may be
because the timing coincided with a wider social acceptance of lesbians
and gay men, which could have led to more workers in learning disability services being 'out' at work. This in turn may have created more
accepting work environments. With the spread of Aids and HIV, there has
also been more urgency to provide good safe sex education for people
with learning disabilities, which necessarily included same gender sex.

I have generally found that relationships between people with learning
disabilities are rarely taken seriously by others. One couple I know had
been engaged for over ten years before their respective services and families supported them to get married. Another woman had a boyfriend for
thirty years; they lived close to each other and their families were friends,
and they also saw each other every day in their day-centre. When his
father suddenly died, he was moved to a different area and no longer
attends the same day-centre. Although efforts have been made by each of
their advocates to get them together from time to time, social services and
day services respectively have not recognized the significance of their
relationship. The result of this bereavement has been that this man is not
only grieving for the loss of his father, but also the loss of the relationship
with his girlfriend; the couple hardly see each other now, and are both
devastated.

When many of us are bereaved of a parent, we seek comfort in our other
relationships, particularly those which are most intimate. As the above
vignette so painfully illustrates, this is rarely a possibility for someone
with a learning disability.

Loss of a child

Many people with learning disabilities long to have a child, but as has already been explored above, this is fraught with difficulties and rarely becomes a reality. Sometimes, sadly, women with learning disabilities become pregnant through abusive, sometimes incestuous relationships, or rape. But some couples with learning disabilities do choose to have a baby. This decision itself can often lead to difficulties. Parents who have learning disabilities are often discriminated against. They are judged by professionals and the general public and are expected to maintain standards of parenting that are not imposed on other parents.

Booth & Booth (1994) cite the term an 'ordinary life' which they quote Towell (1982, in Booth & Booth (1994)) as describing to have come to mean 'a shorthand way of symbolizing the philosophy which should guide the provision of services' (p. 1). They go on to say that for most people, an ordinary life may well include marriage and children, and yet many obstacles are put in the way of this for people with learning disabilities. There are many studies that show high numbers of children are removed from homes where there is a parent with a learning disability (Mickelson 1949, Scally 1973, Accardo and Whitman 1990). Of the twenty families involved in a study conducted by Booth & Booth (1994), fourteen had one or more of their children placed in either short or long term care.

> Child care problems within the family, the admission of a child into care, and the termination of parental rights, cannot be taken at face value as evidence of lack of competence or parenting failure. Such outcomes are often mistakenly attributed to parenting deficiencies when they are more accurately viewed as deficiencies in professional practice, services or supports.
>
> (Booth & Booth 1994, p. 41)

As in many other areas of their lives, most people with learning disabilities are denied adequate knowledge or education in preparation for becoming a parent, and many will not have had good role models within their own families. When they become parents, people with learning disabilities are often living in situations of poverty and debt with poor housing and social isolation. They probably receive little support and if they receive any, it is likely to be inadequate. They may experience victimization and abuse and are probably not served well by the health or welfare services. Is it therefore any wonder that they may experience some problems with parenting? The psychological damage and trauma caused to the entire family by judgemental and rash decisions to remove children from these parents, often resulting in ending contact forever, cannot be underestimated. Booth and Booth (1994) describe their fears for this below:

> In the case of parents with learning difficulties, the value that practitioners place on their parental role may depend on how they value them as people. Where parents are seen as having little or no positive contribution to make to the child's upbringing, they may conclude that the preservation of contact is not in the child's welfare. The dangers of causing avoidable suffering and trauma to parents and children alike by failing to appreciate the nature of the bonds within the family and the capacity of the parents for love and affection (Galliher 1973) are all too real.
>
> (pp.129-130)

I have worked with several women who were referred after the death of parents; when I began to explore their grief with them, what was actually underlying the current grief was the loss of their children, many years earlier. This can complicate grief in a variety of ways. For example, if the dead mother or father was complicit in the decision to have the child or children removed, there can be enormous anger towards the parent who is no longer alive to receive it. This can inhibit grief. There can be an overwhelming sense of aloneness in the world. Children give us some sense of continuity, and this can put people strongly in touch with their own mortality and the finality of death in a way that may feel overwhelming. There can be a strong sense of guilt aroused when, through grieving, the dead parent becomes reinvented as the 'perfect parent' in the person's mind; they then in turn torture themselves, comparing themselves as the poor 'inadequate' parent who could not keep their child.

Loss of friends
Another loss that is so often overlooked is that of friendships. People with learning disabilities often have few opportunities for meeting people. The people who lived for most of their lives in the big institutions may have made some particular relationships after living in the same place with the same people for so long, but on the whole, these relationships were not

taken into account as people were resettled into the community. Decisions were often made on the basis of financial factors. This meant that people were often returned to the borough in which they were living when they had first entered the hospital, and they were likely to have no idea how to contact their old friends from the institution.

For those people living in the community it is a different story, but no less isolating. When they are young they might attend a 'special school'. This is unlikely to be in their own neighbourhood and will draw on a wide catchment area, which makes it difficult for the usual after-school contact that other children enjoy. They will also be more dependent on parents to organize any get-togethers, and this dependency can continue into adult life. When they leave school they may lose contact completely with any friends they had made.

As people with learning disabilities become adults they may attend a day-centre and/or college. From the people that they see every day there may be one who becomes their particular friend; this may or may not be acknowledged by staff and family. However, it is rare for these friendships to develop outside the setting in which they began. In my experience, people with learning disabilities rarely instigate social arrangements outside the situations that are set up for them. This could be due to several factors. They may not have thought that they had any entitlement to ask for things to be any different. They may not be able to ask people back to where they live; they may not know about asking for a friend's telephone number or indeed how to use the telephone, and planning ahead itself may be an unfamiliar concept. One of the saddest aspects of this phenomenon that I often observe is how powerless people with learning disabilities are over whether or not friends remain in their lives or disappear altogether. Often people will have their day at college or the days that they attend the day-centre changed. Or perhaps a decision will be made that they need to move away or change day-centres, and the relationships that the person has within the setting are given little thought.

Loss of staff

A national strategic survey (Wallace 2000) shows that one third of all adults with learning disabilities now live in staffed homes. It is estimated that about a quarter of residential staff in these homes leave their jobs every year (Allen et al 1990). It was quite different within the large institutions, which often had quite a stable staff population. Relationships often blossomed amongst staff, many of whom had left their own homes many miles away to take up work. These relationships often led to 'in-house' marriages. Although many of the large hospitals were built in isolated spots outside towns, residential areas were gradually built up around them in order to house the workers within the institutions. It was common for continuing generations to be employed within the same hospital. This consistency of staffing may have been one of the few positive aspects of the large institutions, although of course this would only be true if the staff-patient relationship was a positive one.

A disturbing finding from research by Landesman-Dwyer and Berkson (1984) highlights the fact that people with severe and profound learning disabilities were extremely vulnerable after a move to the community, because of the change in continuity. The report showed that although these were people who found it difficult to initiate contact with others, many had had clear ties to other residents. These relationships would have been known and recognized by staff who had worked with them for many years, and may well have been facilitated by them. However with the move out of the institutions, the people with more severe learning disabilities had their social interactions disturbed; they often did not find new or lasting relationships, and were at risk of being overlooked altogether. It can take a long time to get to know and build up a relationship with someone with a profound learning disability, and it is therefore not in their best interests to continually experience changes of staff.

In contrast with the large institutions, however, because of the smaller, more intimate nature of a group home, relationships between residents and staff seem to become very important to the people with learning disabilities living in them. Staff are usually given one or sometimes two residents to 'key work'. This role entails an array of complex interactions. At the practical level, it means caring for the person; depending on the degree of disability, this can sometimes involve physically caring, sometimes quite intimately. It also means helping to run the house and all the domestic tasks that this involves, such as shopping, cooking or cleaning, helping people to manage their money and to buy clothes and so on. It also means being an advocate for the person. But this relationship also has a more complex emotional level. Mattison and Pistrang (2000), who carried out research as to what happens when a key worker leaves, interviewed clients about how they saw the role of their keyworker. Their findings fell into three broad categories: those of provider, nurturer and companion. Some descriptions contained accounts of more intense and sometimes sexual feelings towards staff. The researchers add:

> There may be an element of fantasy about these accounts, where clients seem to be wishing for more intimate relationships with their keyworkers. Such fantasies might arise out of clients' confusion about the closeness of the keyworking relationship. (p. 59)

Mattison and Pistrang (2000) also state that: 'Residents seemed appreciative and grateful for having an attachment with someone who seemed to be 'holding them in mind' (p. 61).

As has been mentioned, people with learning disabilities are often very lonely, with few meaningful relationships. Friendships with peers do not often flourish; partly because they are unsupported or unrecognized, but also because the stigma of having a disability is so strong that people do not feel valued themselves, and thus they in turn do not value other people with learning disabilities. This means, as Mattison and Pistrang have said:

> ...for many clients living in residential settings, the keyworker is one of the most important figures in their life, and the relationship between them may be one of the closest clients experience. (2000 p. 2)

It is often therefore of huge significance for people when their key worker leaves or is moved on to key work someone else; yet the ending of these relationships are often overlooked or played down. The impetus for the research that Mattison and Pistrang carried out was driven by the fact that they often received referrals to their psychology department for people with disturbed behaviour. When they investigated a little more fully, it often transpired that a key member of staff had recently left. This corroborates the findings of Emerson back in 1977.

Chapter 6

The use of therapy and counselling

For most people, there is no need to turn to counselling or therapy at a time of bereavement. It is often painful and difficult when someone close to us dies, but most of us cope. We may lean on the friends and family around us, or we may find other ways of coping, such as throwing ourselves into work or taking up where the person we have lost left off. For example, the deceased may have been a keen gardener, and we may find ourselves learning all about gardening and keeping the garden beautiful because it makes us feel closer to that person. However, for a variety of reasons, the process of grieving may become complicated, (see Chapter 3) and in this case we may need to seek professional help. For people with learning disabilities, there are an even greater number of reasons why complications may occur (Hollins & Esterhuyzen 1997, Bonnell & Pascual 1999). It is at this point that a referral for some kind of support should be made to the person's GP (General Medical Practitioner) or to the community team for people with learning disabilities.

Historically, people with learning disabilities have not been considered suitable candidates for the 'talking' therapies. This chapter considers this history, and explores the thinking behind the use of counselling and psychotherapy in various forms with this client group today.

When a referral for bereavement support is made for someone with learning disabilities, a variety of services may be offered. The choice may well depend on which agency the referral is first made to. A GP would be the usual first port of call for anyone at a time of distress through bereavement. A GP's response to a patient experiencing a complicated bereavement would be to either prescribe medication or to refer the person for counselling, or possibly a combination of these approaches. Many GP practices have counsellors attached to their service; however, counselling is usually only offered for a very short period of time. The counsellors may be trained in any one of a number of models of counselling. The likely approaches would be person centered, systemic, or psychodynamic. A GP may also encourage a patient to refer themselves to a counselling or bereavement service in the private or voluntary sector, for longer term counselling.

There are at the present time, however, many barriers of access to either of these two routes to counselling for people with learning disabilities. In the UK, for example, at present, many people with a learning disability are not registered with a GP; some have been relocated from long stay hospitals, and others are elderly people living at home with their families. (One of the key actions in the UK Government White Paper - *Valuing People* (2001) is that by June 2004, all people with a learning disability are to be registered with a GP.) A second barrier can be lack of training and/or experience of working with people with learning disabilities for professionals in this field. This is discussed in more detail later on in this chapter. A third stumbling block may be the preconception that people with learning disabilities will not be able to use therapy or counselling.

If the referral is made to the community team for people with learning disabilities, each professional may have a different approach. The psychologist might offer a brief intervention such as cognitive behavioral therapy, the psychiatrist may offer medication, or the person may be offered a combination of both. Occasionally the person may be referred to an Arts therapist, a psychotherapist or counsellor who specializes in working with people with learning disabilities for a longer-term therapeutic intervention, although these services are a scarce resource. People with learning disabilities have rarely had many options available to them; medication is very often used, and cognitive behavioral therapy is the most likely choice if an intervention is to be offered. These two methods are used with the aim of changing the person's behavioural response rather than with a more long-term aim of trying to work with their distress. A longer-term approach, such as Arts therapy or psychotherapy, would focus on identifying why the person has become 'stuck,' with the aim of moving them forwards and enabling them to gain insight and understanding into themselves and their response to the death.

Holmes (2000) describes psychotherapy in the following way:

The aim of psychotherapy is to help people live more fully in the present – but in order to do so we need to be aware of the past while not being depressively trapped in it, and look forward to the future, without fearing its inherent unpredictability.

(p. 447)

Psychotherapeutic treatments for people with learning disabilities

Historically, non-behavioural psychological treatments, including counselling, psychotherapy and psychoanalysis have rarely been available to people with learning disabilities (Sinason 1992, O'Driscoll 2000) with the occasional exception such as Pierce Clark (1933). Sinason (1992) states that there were a few pockets of interest here and there in the use of psychoanalysis in the field then known as 'mental handicap', but she notes the implication of a divide which occurred between psychoanalysis and psychiatry in the 1940s: 'The advent of non-medical psychoanalysts …meant a dramatic diminishing of the number of analysts who worked in long-stay psychiatric or mental handicap hospitals.' (p. 64) She states that this led to each discipline (psychiatry, psychology, psychotherapy and psychoanalysis) failing to inform the other of developments. America played a leading role in developing psychotherapeutic work with people with learning disabilities in the mid 1940s, although as Sinason (1992) reports, the practitioners were mainly psychologists working psychotherapeutically rather than psychoanalysts or psychoanalytic psychotherapists; so 'their work did not percolate properly through analytic circles' (p. 66).

In the 1960s there were further advances made in France, Canada and the USA, and in the late 1960s and early 1970s there began to be some interest shown in UK. Sinason (1992) describes the level of this interest:

…In 1968, Anna Freud suggested that psychoanalyst Arthur Couch should visit Harperbury Hospital (a long-stay hospital for individuals with a mental handicap, in Radlett, Hertfordshire) in order to explore how handicap affected ego and psychosexual development … However, there had not been any intention in Anna Freud's mind that such patients could or should be offered psychoanalytic treatment.   (p. 70)

Sinason goes on to document a couple of pieces of pioneering work in the 1970s, but it was not really until 1979 with the work of the Tavistock Clinic, and at about the same time, at St George's University Hospital in south London, that there was any significant development in the United Kingdom or Ireland. There were also some fine advances made in the Midlands (UK) by Pat Frankish (1992) and Nigel Beail (1998). The Royal College of Psychiatrists' (RCP) working group in the United Kingdom and Ireland was set up in May 2000 in order to 'examine the present position of psychotherapy in the psychiatry of learning disability and make proposals for future professional and service development' (RCP poster 2002). It states that:

> People with a learning disability are now known to have higher rates of emotional, psychological and psychiatric problems and are more likely to be abused than the general population. Yet up until the last 10-15 years the psychological approaches offered to this client group were almost exclusively behavioural.
>
> (ibid)

However, May 2000 also saw the launch of the new Institute for Psychotherapy and Disability in the UK (Kahr 2000). This signified a small but significant change in attitude towards people with disabilities, if not yet a change in resource and funding. One aspect of the work that has been carried out by the RCP working group is a survey, which aimed to describe the developing pattern of the provision of psychotherapeutic services to people with learning disabilities and identify which professionals provide psychotherapy for this client group and any perceived obstacles to their work. The results of this show that there are a wide range of psychotherapeutic models already being employed by practitioners from a variety of disciplines, and perhaps most importantly, that there is a significant demand for psychotherapeutic services for this client group.

There remain, however, significant barriers to access, including attitudes, lack of appropriate training and supervision. I would add to this list of barriers the perception that psychotherapy is an expensive treatment, and therefore that there are further difficulties in access due to lack of funding. According to Chisholm (1998) and Holmes (2000), psychotherapy is cost-effective over a long-term period because it improves outcome in two crucial ways: patients are symptomatically improved, and their need for other services is reduced. These researchers claim that the amount of psychotropic drugs consumed, visits to the GP, hospital admissions and dependency on benefits, are all reduced. We have noted similar outcomes in our practice. However, this longer-term approach to costing treatment is rarely recognized by health commissioners as a good use of resources with a better outcome for the patient.

Transference and countertransference issues

Transference and countertransference are core concepts of the psychodynamic and psychoanalytic approaches to psychotherapy and counselling. My work is informed by a psychodynamic approach and I have found this to be a highly effective way of working with people with learning disabilities. The next section focuses on this model of working in more depth.

Transference is the process through which a patient displaces feelings onto the therapist which derive from earlier relationships. Countertransference is the term used to describe the conscious and unconscious reactions and feelings of the therapist to the patient and to the transferred feelings from the patient. The therapist uses her/his understanding of these feelings in order to work with the patient. This is particularly important when working with a non-verbal patient, as transference and countertransference are the main tools the therapist has with which to understand the thoughts and feelings of the patient and with which to bring about change. In order for the therapist to be able to use countertransference, it is essential that they can, as Hodges (2003) states:

> ...think about his or her own feelings and prejudices. Supervision and indeed personal therapy can make an essential difference in understanding the very complex emotional relationships created through our clinical work.   (p. 26)

This is why all well-trained therapists and counsellors will have been required to have completed extensive personal therapy whilst in training. There is also a professional requirement for clinical supervision of all case loads, which is a continuing need throughout one's professional career. Psychotherapy can offer the client with learning disabilities the chance to be understood through their entire range of communication, in addition to speech: through body language, creative responses (if using arts-based ways of working) and countertransference. For people who find communicating through words difficult, being listened to in such a different way and being understood (perhaps for the first time) can be a profound experience.

The status of countertransference as a phenomenon associated with counselling or psychotherapy has changed markedly over the years (Thomas 1997). Formal debate on the difficulties connected to countertransference began with Freud (1910). His original view was that 'countertransference arises in the physician as a result of the patient's influence on his unconscious feelings, and we are almost inclined to insist that he shall recognize this counter-transference in himself and overcome it' (p. 144). Here he views it as a hindrance to the psychoanalytic process. Two years later, however, Freud wrote that the analyst must turn his own unconscious like a 'receptive organ' towards the transmitting unconscious of the patient. In other words, as Freud's thinking and ideas progressed he came to view the 'Physician's' unconscious response to the patient as an important analytic tool. These two contrasting thoughts have combined throughout the development of psychoanalytic treatment (Epstein and Feiner 1979). In 1950, Heimann declared 'the analyst's emotional response to his patient…(is) one of the most important tools for his work' (p. 81). Certainly when working with a learning disabled client who has very little speech, it can be the only tool one has for trying to understand their emotional state. It is to this which Hollins (1999) alludes when she states: 'Sometimes as clinicians we have to create hypotheses by observing and understanding human nature, but without diagnostic proof' (p. 7). The only 'proof' we may have is the analysis of our own countertransferential responses.

Hollins (1999), on addressing the value of junior trainee doctors taking a placement in learning disability services states that:

> …they may have to confront uncomfortable and primitive fears about people who are different from themselves. They may even experience some of the stigma which is so powerfully associated with intellectual disability. (p. 11)

These are two important areas to consider, and we may be brought up short by either or both of these experiences at different points in our work with people with learning disabilities. This provides a strong reason for the benefits of working with a psychodynamic awareness with this client group, which can provide an insight into the experience of the person with a learning disability through focussing on and understanding our own unconscious responses. Within this framework we are able to untangle some of the complex dynamics that can arise in relation to working with someone with a disability, and we can begin to understand what feelings belong with whom in a way that might greatly benefit our client. Sinason (1992) refers to Bion's (1959) concept of the analyst as a container; she says,

> The younger the child or the more severely handicapped the child or adult, the greater the need to work more by understanding the countertransference or the nature of the communication the patient has sent to the therapist to hold. (p. 80)

The therapist offers 'containment' through offering a 'safe' space (uninterrupted time, in the same place, at the same time and in a consistent fashion) in which feelings can be expressed consciously or unconsciously by the client. Rather than reacting to the feelings, the therapist thinks about and tries to understand the feelings expressed, in a way that is of use to the client, in order for the client to move forwards. In order for the therapist to contain the client's thoughts and feelings adequately, it is imperative for him or her to have relevant and regular clinical supervision of all casework. Supervision supports the therapist in the task of processing what the client is offering, and enables him or her to separate out any feelings connected to his or her own life from those of the client's.

Thomas (1997) notes that although the full gamut of countertransference reactions may occur when treating a learning disabled client, particular reactions may predominate:

I *Castration anxiety*
Freud used the term castration anxiety very broadly, but mainly as the fear of the loss of a body part. Thomas suggests that for the client, a disability may represent a form of castration. He was mainly focussing on clients with physical disabilities, but if we were to think of castration anxiety as also holding the meaning - fear of loss of potency, as in the 'ability to do' - this is very relevant for the client with a learning disability. He further suggests that all humans have a conscious or

unconscious fear of being damaged, and that the condition of disability in one's client could easily trigger a countertransference response of anxiety in the therapist.

2 *Fear of loss of love*
Thomas (1997) states that the:

> ...therapist's feelings of rejection, loss, or depression when treating patients with disabilities may suggest that the therapist's reactions are accurately mirroring what the patient is feeling.
>
> (p. 153)

As a student training to become a dramatherapist, I remember that I struggled to work with a group of people with learning disabilities. I was on placement, and my task was to run a drama group. Unable to motivate any interest in the group, I reported my feelings of failure and rejection back to my supervision group. Through the supervision I came to realize that my potential 'clients' were a group of wary people. Perhaps they were used to being set up to fail, because like me, other people had often gone to them with expectations of what they could do, and then perhaps not thought of adapting the task in order to make it accessible, resulting in the project failing. This sort of experience can happen over and over again for people with learning disabilities, and the people working with them. It seemed that possibly years of this sort of experience had left the group unwilling to take a risk with me.

It became clear that my first task was thus not to concentrate on making the drama happen, but to empower the group in order that they felt safe enough to risk experimenting creatively with me. Once I took this on board, it became possible to work with them. Initially, I told the group that I was feeling unsure whether or not they wanted to be doing drama with me; it felt important that I aired some of the feelings that I felt were in the room. Some people said that they did want to, but that other people 'would muck about' or 'spoil it'; the thought that I might spoil things remained unspoken. This discussion led me to suggest that we make some ground rules as to how we should all work together. We worked on these together and continued the process at the beginning of the next few sessions. I wrote the ground rules down for the group. I made sure that I found a way to engage every member of the group in the process of negotiating the rules. These were brought out at every session, and anyone in the group could remind any other group member, or me, of the rules, if any of us started to lapse.

By bringing some of the concerns of the group out into the open, and through making the rules, the atmosphere in the room completely changed. Addressing the group's fears in this way, and giving group members a tool through which to take control, (the rules), seemed to free people up, and they were able to go on to do some very creative work. I had been supported by the supervision process to understand the group's anxieties as well as my own; by recognising my counter-transference to their fear of failure and their fear of my rejection of them, I was able to address this, which resulted in freeing the group from lethargy and myself from my own feelings of rejection.

3 Fear of loss of the object

In psychoanalytic terms 'object' means a person or thing to which the client is very attached; that to which the person-as-subject directs their feelings or action. The therapist can begin to fear the client becoming very dependent in him or her.

4 Fear of death

The therapist's awareness of thier own mortality may be heightened by a client who is very in touch with the 'societal death wish'. They can also become painfully conscious of the 'social death' that many clients will experience. These thoughts may raise feelings of guilt in the therapist. Both these fears (3 & 4) are crucial to have in mind during bereavement therapy with people with learning disabilities. Both are connected to fear of loss through death, one's own and a loved one's. In light of society's death wish (as discussed in Chapter 2), the fear of death can be very strong unconsciously. Fear of loss of the object (see above) may be accentuated by the real death of a parent, but is also crucial to consider in the light of dependence. All people with learning disabilities will be dependent on others for certain aspects of their life, to a greater or lesser degree. The experience of dependency is usually less one of reciprocal dependency than for someone without a dis-ability, although this is sometimes not the case. Death of a parent may well have stirred up painful issues around dependency, and there may be many questions over who will now be providing support for the client, and anger and other complex feelings connected to this (see Chapter 5)

5. Fear of self-disintegration

This is very common when working with people with learning disabilities, who may find it very difficult to think, and who may have a fragmented sense of self from a constantly interrupted dialogue with their primary carer during early development. The therapist can experience the disintegration of their own thinking.

Thomas goes on to say;

> ...In addition to these psychodynamic responses, therapists may expect to experience many of the same situational, socio-cultural, and historical reactions to disability as other persons.
>
> (p. 156)

Marks (1999) refers to psychoanalytic theorists such as Kohon, 1986; Raynor, 1991; Symington, 1986, and Gomez, 1997, who place emphasis on real experiences in the social environment shaping the psyche. She describes different levels of 'external reality'; these may be interpersonal relationships, such as those between the mother and her infant, family dynamics or influences from and within wider groups, and also influences from popular culture. She says, 'The insights of psychoanalysis can be used to look at disability at the socio-cultural, institutional, group and interpersonal levels as well as on the intra-psychic level' (p. 20).

The **roc** Loss and Bereavement service, mentioned in the Introduction, uses elements of systemic psychotherapy to inform its practice, as well as working from a psychodynamic perspective. Systemic psychotherapy takes account of the network around the individual, which it sees as influencing, holding and reflecting internal parts of the client.

An example of this is demonstrated by describing a client who worked hard in therapy to show me the 'able' side of himself. He was very gifted numerically, and often impressed me with his skill in this area. Meanwhile the staff team supporting him, and on whom he was very dependent, often got the dates of sessions wrong, arrived late and generally 'held' the dysfunctional aspects of the client. I worked with the staff team to help them to recognize what was happening, and they strove to support him in a less disabling way. As he felt more empowered in his day-to-day life, he became less defensive in thinking about what it was like to have a disability; he was able to express his anger and frustration at this. He was able to think more clearly about the changes in his life since his bereavement and to make choices about how he would like to live in the present and the future. (For a longer account of work with this client, see Chapter 10)

roc as a service believes that it is important to be able to communicate and think about such things through a whole 'system' approach, in order to enable long term change to come about.

Insight

Bicknell (1983) suggests that insight into having a disability and the implications of this is far more present in people with learning disabilities than has often been believed. She states that it is linked to their cognitive ability and also to their life experience. She adds:

> Insight is also linked with failure to reach self-imposed standards. The mentally handicapped child in a large sibship often imposes standards that are just above the younger sibling. Somebody must be less capable than him. Families can be warned that there may be problems when the younger sibling of normal intelligence overtakes the handicapped older sibling.
>
> (p. 173)

She goes on to suggest that if we are really to understand the meaning of handicap beyond simply the organic meaning, we need to ask -

- what does it mean for *this* person?
- to have *this* handicap?
- at this time in his/her life?
- with this caretaker?
- in this environment?
- and in this peer group?

If we can find answers to these questions for the people with whom we are working, we will have far greater understanding of the insight that they have into their disability and what it means for them. People will often develop defensive reactions to the insight into their own disability (Bicknell 1983, Sinason 1992, Thomas 1997 & Marks 1999). These defences can further disable the person. However, research indicates that defensive behaviour will often stop within the first year of therapy (Carlsson et al. 2002). This has an important implication in the debate over why long term therapy is often a better treatment model for people with learning disabilities; the fact is that it can take some time for long-term defences to come down, in order that deeper work can take place. Ending therapy too early can leave a client with learning disabilities in the vulnerable position of having recognized their defensive coping mechanisms and perhaps a feeling of having been 'found out', but without any further work on ego-strengthening or developing the ability to think.

We can see a very clear example of defensive coping skills in Neville Symington's (1981) moving account of psychotherapeutic treatment with a patient whom he calls Harry Smith. He describes Harry's preoccupation with his own intelligence and how he becomes aware of the mixed messages he has received. His father, on the one hand, had placed him as extremely able, and the manager of his day-centre, on the other, thought that Harry was not very capable at all. When asked by Symington how he would measure himself, Harry places himself just below average. During the course of the analysis, it emerges that Harry had been travelling unaccompanied to his sessions for several weeks, something which he was unable to do at the start of the process. Symington says,

> I then acknowledged with him that he was more intelligent than people took him for. I then pointed out to him very firmly that he must be pulling the wool over people's eyes. He agreed with this and wondered why it was. In the same context we got to the fact that he clowned a great deal so that people laughed at him and thought him more of a fool than he was.   (p. 191)

Symington goes on to interpret that Harry felt there was something wrong with him, and that he was extremely anxious in case people laughed at him because of this. So he exaggerated the process, and was then able to feel that he was really perfectly alright. But what caused him pain and anxiety was that there really was something wrong. This type of defensive exaggeration has been termed by Sinason (1992) as 'secondary handicap', which she developed from Freud's (1910) original concept of 'secondary gain'. Freud originally used this this term to describe how a patient might exaggerate their symptoms to their advantage. In people with learning disabilities, we may often see this manifest in a phenomenon which Sinason names the 'handicapped smile', '...(for)... adults who know they are not wanted, smiling is a way of paying to stay alive' (p. 143): or as opportunistic handicap, 'where every destructive aspect of the self finds a home in the disability' (p. 2).

The therapist needs to be able to keep in mind the loss or pain that a client may feel in connection with having a disability. The client may or may not be able to verbally acknowledge this. It is all too easy for the therapist to collude with the defensive behaviour of the client. It is a fine balance to find between being gently supportive of the learning disabled client, and making demands on him or her to think. One of the most common defences that a person with a learning disability will employ against the knowledge of disability is to not think (Simpson 2002), and yet when a therapist enables the client with mild to moderate learning disabilities to do so, room for personal growth is created alongside the pain of the insight into the disability.

Considerations for the therapist or counsellor working with a learning disabled client.

Every client is unique and will demand something different from us but there are particular issues that should be considered when taking on a client with a learning disability.

Communication – from concrete to symbolic

It is essential that the therapist is sensitive to all the different ways in which the client is communicating, and that the client is allowed to dictate the pace. It will be important to assess the forms of communication that the client is most comfortable with using. Does she use verbal communication? Can you understand what she says? Speech may be unclear for physical reasons. For example, people with Down syndrome are born with an extra large tongue. If they are given speech therapy when they are young, they may develop clear speech, but if they have not had this opportunity, it may take time to get used to understanding what they are saying.

Many people with a learning disability are also born with sensory impairments. It can be important to ask about these before beginning an assessment as this may influence the therapist's approach to communication. It may be helpful to simplify the language used, and to back this up with signs and symbols. Displaying warmer affect than usual, and sometimes slightly exaggerating your facial expressions can both be useful, as it is not always easy for people with learning disabilities to read body language or ambiguous expressions.

Some people may talk very little; this may be due to lack of confidence or low self-esteem. The person may not have been in situations before where he or she has been expected to have an opinion, or to express his or her thoughts or feelings. For others, this may have gone one stage further and they may have become electively mute. This can come about through years of not being listened to, or perhaps in response to something traumatic that has happened, such as abuse. None of this means that the person will not understand what is said to them, and it is important not to give up on communicating and to still talk to the person and share thoughts and ideas with them.

Some people may talk a lot, and although it is possible to hear clearly the words that they are saying, it may be difficult to make sense out of what is being said (see the case of Philip below). The person's thinking may be fragmented due to the organic nature of the disability, their life experience, or a combination of both.

It will be important to assess the level of understanding (emotional and cognitive maturity) the client has. For example, is the person able to understand what is being said on a basic level? Can he or she follow a simple instruction, such as "*Would you like to hang your coat up*"? If they appear not to be able to follow this, it needs to be clarified whether this is because of anxiety or lack of confidence, whether the person has not understood the therapist because he or she is new to them, or because they do not understand the instruction itself.

It is then important to find out whether the client can move beyond 'concrete' thinking. Abstract images and concepts are often used in therapy, but this may be very confusing for a client with a learning disability. The therapist may need to begin by communicating using very concrete language, and then find ways to enable the person to move beyond this to a more developed way of thinking and communicating. Using other media often helps. Drawing and pictures are useful; the therapist may use simple symbols to back up what she has said or to explore issues. The client may be encouraged to express how they are feeling or what they are thinking about through drawing, painting, poetry or stories (Blackman 1999, 2000, 2002, Read 1999a, 1999b).

Puppets or dolls can be used to help the client tell a story or to express something difficult. Traditional stories may be used in order to explore issues from personal stories more fully (Gersie 1991, Blackman 1999). (These techniques are explored more fully in the following chapter). Personal photos, pictures from magazines and specially created resources such as the *Books Beyond Words* series or some of the picture packs (see Resource List) may be helpful. However, it is important to remember as Hollins (1999) points out when describing the creation of the first *Book Beyond Words* (Gaskell/St. George's Hospital Medical School):

> Our search for non-verbal means of communication did not mean that one should not talk to people who have been bereaved, or should not offer them sympathy and understanding. But, for some, words provided no comprehensible explanation. We found that explanations and comfort could be provided through pictures, and through personal photographs.   (p. 3)

The use of these sorts of techniques can allay some of the anxiety caused by the imagined expectations of a more formal verbal approach. In some cases it may be pertinent to invite trustworthy advocates to accompany the client into sessions in order that they can support communication. The key is to be as flexible as possible.

Knowledge

There may be many gaps in the client's knowledge, depending on the extent of the learning disability, formal education and inclusion in family decisions and rituals. As with any client, it is important not to make assumptions about the person's life experience. It is extremely helpful to do as much research as possible about a client's life. It may be difficult for the person with a learning disability to tell the therapist very much. This may be because they are not used to speaking about themselves, or because verbal communication is limited. The therapist can help her client to disclose more if she has some sense of their life already; this will mean that she can ask relevant questions, and pick up on the tiniest of clues that are given to her. But even if she has researched and thinks that she knows quite a bit about her client's life, it is essential not to assume that one can ever really know how it actually was. It is impossible, for example, to imagine the experience of having been left in a large noisy hospital as a small child of seven, in a strange and frightening environment which then becomes your home with your parents only visiting at weekends, if at all. It is always important to listen to our client's own description of their experiences, whether these are given through their actions or their words.

Much of the kind of research that I refer to could be general reading up on the history of lives in the big institutions, rather than being specific to your client's own life story. However, it is sometimes helpful to know specific details about a client's life, if, for example, one is concerned that the client will be unable to disclose the information for him or herself because of difficulties in communication. This is a very different situation to working with other client groups, and therefore needs a considered approach. I always let clients know all the information that I was given at the time of referral, and who gave me this information. Sometimes further on into the therapy, if there is a gap in the client's knowledge or memory, I ask them if they would like me to see if I could find out some more information. This can be done by the therapist alone or with the client present. If the person has a social worker, they may be able to help.

It is also sometimes possible to access peoples' files from long stay hospitals. Unfortunately, many hospitals destroyed people's files when they closed down, but this is not the case for everyone. A website has been developed by David O'Driscoll that could be useful in this research (wwwlearningdisabilityhistory.com). An important factor to bear in mind if accompanying someone to read their file is that the language used to document information is often very outdated and judgmental, and can be upsetting. It is important to prepare people for this and to read ahead a little bit so that you are also prepared.

Confidentiality
Setting simple ground rules with the client in the first session is helpful; this can help the client begin to know what to expect from therapy, and if negotiated, can form the beginning of an empowering relationship. The ground rules should include:

• when the sessions will take place, including the timing and the duration

- that the sessions are a place where feelings can be expressed, such as sadness or anger
- a clarification of what will and will not be shared with people outside the sessions

Such discussion is useful as people with learning disabilities often experience a multitude of people speaking about them in intimate detail, without asking for permission and often without including them in the conversation, even if they are present. This is a difficult issue, because it is important that information that is helpful to the person with a learning disability is passed to whoever is supporting them, but perhaps the way in which this is done needs to be given more consideration. Is it possible to involve the person themselves in the process of information transfer, for example? Kahr (1996) has written of benign or malignant breaks of confidentiality. He describes *benign breaks* as those which are intended to help the client, whereas *malignant breaks* take the form of gossiping or passing on information inappropriately.

When introducing the concept of confidentiality, the therapist might say, for example, that nothing will be shared without the client's knowledge and/or consent. The therapist might also include the client in thinking about what sort of things it might be helpful for carers to know about, if anything (for example if the client has said in the session that they feel sad that they never visit their mother's grave, then it might be helpful for staff to know this in order that they can support the person to make a visit).

A further groundrule is needed about safety, self-harm, abuse and hurting others, stating that if any of these things are disclosed, the therapist has a duty to tell carers, and that the client will be informed that this will happen. The therapist needs to state that even if the client does not give consent for this disclosure, the therapist will have to go ahead and make a report.

Suggestibility

There may be a propensity to suggestibility for some clients with a learning disability. This may partly stem from a desire to please and therefore to give a 'right' answer, or it might come from a fear of getting something wrong and thus failing. It is therefore important for the therapist to be aware of any signals that they may give towards a particular answer or statement, and to think carefully as to how questions are worded; they need to be impartial.

As has already been explored elsewhere in this book, many people with learning disabilities will have experienced insecure early attachments. They may also have experienced a lifetime of failure and lack of acknowledgment and expectation. In an excellent article on working with sexually abused children with learning disabilities, Allington-Smith et al (2002) state that:

> We should not expect children who have been severely admonished for their slowness to make therapeutic attachment and treatment progress at the same rate as their more able peers. Their ability to think without anxiety will have been impaired by a history of failure and subsequent criticism...   (p. 68)

They go on to say:

> A posture of openness and willingness to accept and understand each particular child's confusion and anxiety is often sufficient in itself as a starting point for building a therapeutic alliance.
>
> (ibid)

This applies just as well with adults with learning disabilities.

As Sinason (1992) warns us, 'To reach and explore this emotional intelligence a great deal of guilt must be dealt with, guilt of the patient for his handicap and guilt of the worker for being normal' (p. 74). As I have already stressed, it is therefore imperative to have good, regular clinical supervision, in order that the weight of this potential guilt can be shared and countertransference issues be understood.

Philip is a man with severe learning disabilities in his early forties, referred after the death of his mother; his father had died some years previously. Philip had also witnessed the long-stay hospital in which he had lived for many years being pulled down around him; as he was moved into a new bungalow on the same site. This meant that he had also seen many staff leave. Philip had experienced a form of physical lameness as a child, which had required a lot of medical treatment and separations from his family at a young age. Although he was verbal, he had difficulties with communication and often appeared muddled and confused. Philip had not attended either of his parents' funerals.

He had been referred to the bereavement service because he had become obsessive about losing or breaking any of his possessions, to the extent that a shed had been built in the garden of his bungalow for him to lock away his possessions. Staff were also finding him very difficult to deal with, as he would often ask very direct questions about death, to which they felt ill-equipped to respond. It was hoped that through bereavement therapy, Philip would be able to get some answers to his questions about death and that he might be able to work through his fears of losing things that were important to him.

In our early sessions together, it was difficult to understand what Philip was saying a lot of the time, but there were snatches of dialogue which sounded as though he was repeating the kind of conversations he may have heard. I often had the distinct impression, in fact, that this is what he was doing. Sometimes he appeared to be scolding himself. I was subsequently informed that Philip's father was very strict with him. Sometimes these monologues were about politics or building work. Whenever he chose to use creative materials in the sessions, such as paint, he would use them in a very practical workman-like style, often telling me details about how to care for or use the materials. These seemed to be skills that he might have learned from his father. I sensed as time went on that these were techniques that Philip had developed in order to keep his father alive for him in some way. Although he had been referred following his mother's death, it seemed that he was at present more preoccupied with his father.

I began to explore this theory with Philip. I focused on direct reminiscences with him about his father. We compiled a book together with pictures and I scribed (wrote down) memories for him composed of fragments recalled here and there of time spent with his father. As this work progressed, his dialogue became more lucid and he appeared much calmer; he also became more able to cope with small changes in his life. During this work I was very aware that Philip made hardly any reference to his mother at all, and then only when prompted. I discovered that his mother had been physically disabled and that this had meant that his father had to take on a lot of the caring role in Philip's family. The few memories that he shared of his mother were in connection to food.

Further into the therapy Philip developed a keen interest in the sand tray which stands in my practice room. He began very tentatively at first to 'play' with the dry sand; he then discovered that water could be mixed with it. He did this again in a very workmanlike way; at this point, the *activity still seemed to have a connection to his father. Gradually over the weeks, this activity changed in quality. He became more experimental and more playful, and it seemed important to him that I was witnessing him. I began to feel like a mother watching her young child at play, and I sometimes gave a little bit of a commentary. This seemed to be a time in the work where memories of his own mother began to be more present for him.*

When he was experimenting with the sand, it provided me with an opportunity to ask whether his mother baked cakes, as he looked somewhat as if this was what he was doing. This prompted him to reminisce about his mother in the kitchen of his family home, which led on to further memories of her preparing the Sunday roast with Philip collecting mint for the sauce or vegetables that his father had grown for her to prepare. It seemed as though by witnessing him as he engaged in early sensory play, I may have provided the right environment for him to remember early experiences with his mother. The two important ingredients seemed to be gentle psychological 'holding' and a sensory activity. The sensory play may also have provided him with an opportunity to experience some of the sort of early experimentation processes necessary for a healthy developing child. This perhaps had not been available to him in early childhood, due to his mother's ill health and his own hospitalisation.

For Philip it was always difficult to work reflectively (ie for him to be able to think about his feelings or consider any of my tentative analysis in the sessions). It seemed unlikely that he had the intellectual capacity for such work. But through the activity-based approach that I mainly adopted in my work with him, he helped me to understand something about his relationships with each of his parents. This enabled me to work through the transference of these relationships, in order to free Philip up from his rather preoccupied previous state. In the sessions I learned that he had a strong internalisation of his father, and a weaker sense of his mother. This may have represented his relationship with each of them. I had the sense that Philip's father had been the person in the family who had 'managed' him by being firm, but also by passing on useful skills and keeping him occupied. His mother on the other hand had perhaps not been physically able to take much care of him; he had also experienced a lot of early separation from her due to his own physical disability.

Towards the end of the intervention, a member of staff died at Philip's day service. Philip went to the funeral; the first he had ever attended.

This was a turning point for him. He now became very curious about his own parents' funerals and quite indignant that he had not been allowed to attend them. He talked about how sad everybody had been at the funeral, and how many people had been there. I suggested that he could still have something like a funeral to say goodbye to his own parents, and he liked this idea. We began to plan a memorial service for his mother and father. He chose to hold it in the garden of his house, and decided that he was going to plant a walnut tree. (He had frequently referred to a walnut that he remembered from childhood. There had also been one at the long stay hospital where he had spent so many years). He decided that he would invite his sisters to come to the service. We made contact with the local vicar and over the next few sessions, Philip planned what he wanted included in the service. He dictated to me several memories of time spent with his parents that he wanted the vicar to read out loud, and he chose the hymn which we practised singing. The service was held on a beautiful sunny day, both his sisters attended and the staff in his house provided a feast for afterwards.

This experience really seemed to have a profound experience on Philip. He had experienced the reverence of a ritualised goodbye to his parents, and he had been able to take control over this process. Over the course of this piece of work, Philip became less and less anxious. He was slightly less fixated on the fear of losing his possessions, he became quieter and more reflective, and he was more focused and easier to communicate with. The therapy had provided him with somewhere to make some sort of sense of his chaotic feelings since so many major changes and losses had occurred in his life. These had been explored through making a memory book, in order to contextualise some of his former verbal chaos. I had felt that this was linked to the loss of his father, the father who had given Philip order and structure whilst he was alive. It seemed to me that Philip was now searching for this by repeating fragments of familiar pieces of his father's dialogue. The developmental play with the sand seemed to enable him to access memories and feelings about his mother. And finally Philip had been given the chance to say goodbye to both of his parents, in a way that felt right for him.

Chapter 7

Therapeutic interventions

This chapter is primarily written from the point of view of supporting a person with a learning disability, bereaved by the death of a parent, within the context of a counselling or therapeutic relationship. I believe this particular kind of bereavement often carries with it the most intricate and multi-layered complications, but the process can, of course, be used as a model for considering any other sort of bereavement. There are a variety of ways a bereaved person may be supported when they are grieving. Counselling or therapy will only be necessary if a person is finding it difficult to cope with bereavement. Sometimes it is enough for carers to provide informal support. Some of the interventions described here could be used outside the therapeutic framework, so long as confidentiality and safe practice (such as obtaining clinical supervision) are observed.

Assessing the need for support
Throughout this book, I have referred to the many elements to be taken into account when trying to understand the impact of bereavement and the specific issues that might complicate bereavement for someone with a learning disability. In Chapter 1, I examined different models that have been developed in order to understand the individual and the complex process of mourning. I have drawn on some of these models, in particular those of Le Poidevin, Shuchter, Zisook, Stroebe and Schutt, to develop an assessment model specific to the complexities of the situation for many bereaved people with learning disabilities.

As people supporting this client group, I believe that it is important for us all to keep a constantly open and inquiring mind about the varying factors within our client's circumstances which may hinder the process of grief, and those which may help. Our clients may or may not be able to provide us with all of the answers directly. But if we bear these factors in mind and do not make assumptions, the search for this information may enable us to guide our client towards a positive way of coping with grief. Very often, bereaved people simply need the people around them to be sensitive, considerate, and have some straightforward awareness of the process of mourning. However, for a person with a learning disability, an ongoing assessment of the individual's specific situation will enable carers and professionals to make an informed decision, in partnership with the bereaved person wherever possible, as to whether they are in need of specialised support through their bereavement, or not.

Model for assessing grief responses for a person with learning disabilities

Emotional responses	•Does this individual recognize their own emotions? •Can they express their emotion? •How does the environment around them respond to their expression of emotion?
Cognitive understanding	•Does this individual have an understanding of the concept of death? •Does this person have an understanding of the permanence of their new situation? •If the death was expected, did the person have an understanding of this?
Social responses	•Was the person informed of the expected death? •Has the individual been informed of the death? •Were they informed immediately? By whom; how?
Social impact	•What significance has this loss had on the person's familial network? •What significance has this loss had on their social network (day centre, work, college and so on)? •What has the impact of the loss been on other members of the social/familial network?

Developed from the work of Le Poidevin, Shuchter, Zisook, Stroebe and Schutt

	•What changes in status or role have to be negotiated? (by the child, the carer, the mother, the wife & so on) •What support, and what quality of support is available?
Physical	•What has the impact been on the person's physical health?
Lifestyle	•Has this loss meant a move from the family home? •Has this meant more than one move? •Has this person experienced other significant losses? •What other lifestyle changes has this created?
Continuing the relationship with the deceased	•Did this person see the deceased shortly before they died? •Did this person attend the funeral? •Does this person have access to photos and mementoes of the deceased? •Is this person able to visit the grave if there is one? •Is this person able to reminisce with others who knew the deceased?
Changes in functioning	•Has this person's ability to communicate with others been affected by this loss? •Has this person lost any skills since this bereavement?
Spiritual	•In what ways has this bereavement affected this person's religious or other spiritual belief systems? •If this person was part of a local religious community/congregation, are they still able to keep these links? •What meaning have they ascribed to this loss?
Changes in identity	•To what extent has the loss affected the individual's self-concept and self-esteem?

The answers to the questions on the previous pages should give a good picture as to which areas of life the person is coping with, and which they are most struggling with at the moment. It will also aid consideration as to how best to support this person in adjusting to life without the deceased.

The way in which to carry out this assessment will vary according to the individual and their circumstances. For some people, it may be appropriate to ask some of the questions directly, or to assess the person's knowledge by using pictures and discussion. This could be carried out in two or three structured interviews by a social worker or other appropriate professional. Work with a person with more severe learning disabilities would need a different approach; these questions could be addressed over a period of time. Some of the answers may be gathered from people who know the individual well, some may be observed. Others (such as the question regarding the understanding of the death concept) may need to be specifically assessed using tools such as books (see Resource List) or props. Dead insects may be used to ascertain the individual's understanding of the permanence of death, for example.

It is important that all answers are written up and stored together with the person's other records. This assessment should inform all decisions taken with or on behalf of the individual with regard to their future, and should be used as an ongoing reference point which can be updated. It must be stressed that an assessment on its own is a pointless exercise. It is only useful if the information gathered is used constructively.

I recently co-wrote a bereavement policy for an assessment and treatment service. Part of this involved gathering an individual's loss history as they entered the service. We indicated a variety of ways for this to be done, which included: gathering information from previous records, interviewing the person with learning disabilities themselves where possible, as well as family and/or other individuals such as previous staff. An assessment like the one above could be adapted for this purpose.

Learning to live without the deceased

In addition to supporting the person through the process of grief, families and professionals need to think about how we can empower the bereaved person to develop in their life generally, and in particular to consider what strengths and interests the person with learning disabilities has which can be encouraged and built upon. If the loss has been that of a parent, there may be issues of dependency specific to having been the child in the family with a disability, for example. These will affect self-esteem, self-confidence and self-image. Stroebe and Schut's (1996) Dual Process Model (see Chapter 1) may be very useful to consider here in terms of the work of restoration orientation. However 'restoration' may be considered a misnomer in some cases, as it may be the first time that anyone has actively supported the person to build up their self-esteem and to develop a positive sense of self.

It will be important to think of this process as fluid, since, with each move towards growth and independence, there may be huge emotional responses towards the deceased parent. Sinason (1992) has described the process which can often occur between a parent and their disabled child, where the parent perceives a need to keep their disabled offspring preserved in the state of perpetual childhood (see also Chapter 5). The infantalised bereaved adult may swing between rage at the deceased parent for having maintained this state for so long, denying their psycho-sexual maturation, and clinging to this state in terror of having to grow up and take on responsibilities. Such clinging may also serve as a way of holding onto or continuing the bond with the deceased parent.

It is important that everyone in the supporting network surrounding a bereaved person with a learning disability is aware that they will have an influence over how the person's link is maintained with the deceased. This may simply be through the way they refer to the deceased, or, indeed, whether they make mention of the dead person at all. So, for example, if someone is clearly reluctant to buy anything new to wear, they may be thinking to themselves, *"I don't think my Mum would like me in this type of thing; we used to shop in different sort of shops"*. A sensitive supporter would perhaps recognize that this sort of internal dialogue might be occurring and instead of becoming exasperated at not being able to find anything that the person will agree to buy, they may open the dialogue; *"I wonder what colour your Mum would have chosen with you?"*.

As I have already pointed out, the internal construction of the deceased is an important part of the grieving process. For someone with a learning disability, there may be a variety of impediments to this:

- The person may have difficulties with their short or long-term memory; this could be connected to the learning disability
- They may not have access to any photos or mementoes
- The person may no longer be in the same physical location and

therefore not have the environmental stimuli around them to trigger reminiscence
- They may not have access to other people to talk to who knew the deceased
- The attitude of other people may be unhelpful. For example, they may be constantly 'jollied along'

As Klass et al (1996) point out: 'We cannot ignore that we are talking about connections that, in part, depend on the memory and the ability of the survivor to maintain an inner dialogue. This ability changes with stages of development' (p. 350). In order to enable a person to grieve, they suggest that the professional/helper can focus on what sort of support the person has access to, educate the person about the range of 'appropriate' grieving behaviours, help the person to know how to use their inner strength, how to use community resources to facilitate coping, and also facilitate the survivor's construction of a bond with the deceased.

I have emphasized the importance of helping a bereaved person to build their self-esteem and also to maintain a link to the deceased. I will now look at two specific interventions with which to do this.

Reminiscence and building life-story books

A useful way of beginning the work of developing and strengthening a bond with the deceased is through reminiscence. This also enables the person with learning disabilities to develop a sense of identity and to discover their likes and dislikes, strengths and weaknesses, with the supportive presence of another person.

It is our past and our memories that help to form our sense of self. Many people with learning disabilities will have experienced very fragmented lives. They may have had many separations from their parents and the home environment due to respite care or stays in hospital. Some people will have left home, sometimes at a very young age, to live in a long stay hospital or a community home, and may have experienced several changes of residential placements over the years.

For many of these people, it will be difficult for them to carry a sense of their own history. This may be due in part to difficulties with memory and sequencing, but also to a lack of personal possessions and unfamiliar environments, which might provide cues for remembering. It may also be excruciatingly painful to remember, preferable perhaps to numb all thinking.

For someone who has lived in a long stay hospital most of their life, there will have been no place for personal possessions or photographs. The wards were crowded, and all the personal space that was provided was a tiny bedside cupboard. Nothing was safe from other people: even clothes were shared up until a decade or so ago. People were often moved from ward to ward, so developing a sense of belonging was almost impossible.

Others who have lived at home all their lives may have relied on their family to do their thinking and remembering for them. When they suddenly find themselves living away from the family home with staff who know very little about them, with perhaps one parent dead and the other with dementia, their experience may have much in common with that of a refugee who has no history and little ability to convey their own life experience to any one. Scenarios like this unfortunately are only too common.

Reminiscence is the process of recalling the past (Butler 1963) and it is an important part of making sense of one's life. This can happen spontaneously and is a natural part of most of our lives; it can be a shared activity or an unspoken solitary process.

People with learning disabilities have often had very little control over the course of relationships they do make. Friends, family and staff members come and go. The process of reminiscing in a more formal context, either one-to-one or in a group, can be helpful in that it can enable someone to build a sense of their life story, which in turn helps to build a stronger sense of identity.

I have already mentioned the role of reminiscence in helping to build an internal link with the deceased, and this is often a good starting point. It is important, however, to recognize that reminiscing can be painful. As I mentioned, many people have cut off from painful experiences in their lives by not thinking, and this needs to be taken into account when embarking on the work with anyone in which connections to the past may be re-made. It is important to have their consent and to negotiate some ground rules. Such rules should include realistic points about confidentiality, for example what would happen if the person disclosed abuse. Another ground rule might say that the individual or a group-member need only speak if they wish. It is also important for workers to consider what emotional and practical support he or she can set up for him or herself, as it is not always easy to listen to someone's painful experiences.

Obviously if this work is undertaken within a therapeutic context this will already be in place, but in any other context this must be carefully considered.

It is important to note that some people are not natural reminiscers. It may be important for their own psychological survival *not* to think of the past. For a person like this, who has perhaps experienced trauma, I would work in a different way. It is imperative that no-one is ever forced to reminisce. This being said, when reminiscence is successful, it can often prove to be a most uplifting experience to rediscover with someone their past life, and to enable them to make sense of their past in the context of the life that they are living now.

Creating a life-story book

A good way to begin to reminisce with someone on a one-to-one basis is to compile a life-story book. This gives the reminiscing a format and a goal. Life-story books can take a wide variety of forms, individual to the person whose story it tells. The most important points to remember are:

- To use a loose-leaf format in order that the book can continually be added to, and so that the sequence is flexible
- To start at the point at which the person feels comfortable (which may not be way back when they were very young, or in remembering the deceased)

I will use the general term 'supporter' in the following section to refer to the counsellor, therapist, reminiscence worker or care worker who may be supporting the person to make a life-story book.

Once the person has agreed to make a life-story book, it is important to let them decide where they would like to begin. They may already have shared some reminiscences prior to starting, which could now be worked on to become pages in the book. They may be encouraged to bring photos or other pieces of memorabilia to the sessions, which can lead to a starting point, or they may have clear ideas of their own. Whichever it is, it is important to let them begin with what feels comfortable to them. As the work gets underway, it becomes easier for the memories to flow, but it is often not until a lot of pages have been constructed that any chronological order becomes apparent. It is important not to get too fixated on the idea of having a perfect story from birth through to the present time. The reality will be that there will only be time together to do so much. The points that have been covered will be good enough. The process of making a life-story book is just as important as the finished product, as reminiscing safely with an attentive other seems to help to start up the process of allowing memories to flow.

Careful thought needs to be given to the storage of the book while it is 'in progress'. It is often best for the supporter to keep it in between sessions, as otherwise it can get lost or forgotten and become difficult to work on. The supporter needs to have a safe place for it to live, where it will be kept confidential (the person whose book it is needs to know this). This should be in a locked room or cupboard.

When the structured work on the life storybook ends, it is important to stress to the person that this is not necessarily the end of the book, and that it can be added to at any time. It is a good idea not to make the book too neat and tidy, but to think of it more like a scrapbook. If it is too 'finished-looking' or done in a style that may be difficult for someone else to copy, it will be hard for anyone else to feel comfortable about supporting the person to keep adding to it. The ending of the work together will be the time at which the book is handed over to the individual to keep. Some preparatory work should be done with the person about where they are going to keep the book safe, about who they would like to share it with, who they would not like to share it with, and how this will be managed.

The cover

In preparation for this work together, the person can be encouraged to make a front-cover for their book, so that it really begins to become their own. Indeed, the life-story book could become very important to the person, particularly if they have very few other meaningful possessions. This book could become a way for the person with learning disabilities to share something of themselves with others, if they so choose. Alternatively, it may be just a personal and private chance to reflect and reminisce on their own life at different times in the future. I know of one man who made a book when he was in therapy with me. He now has the book at home and keeps it in his room. He looks at it or adds to it when he is feeling in need of a connection with his family. He also uses it as an aid when he wants to share thoughts about his family with staff in his home, particularly when he is feeling low. Walter (1996) emphasises the importance of talking to others about the deceased in his biographical model of grief. He argues that:

> ...conversations with others help bereaved people to construct a durable biography that enables them to integrate the relationship into their ongoing lives. (p. 7)

Other reminiscence tools
Photos
If the person has access to photographs from their past this is obviously an easy starting point for reminiscence. If the person can describe the photo a little, or make a few connections, the supporter can write down as much as possible and ask prompt questions. For example, if the photographs were taken on holiday, one could ask where the holiday took place, who else went, how they got there, what the weather was like, what they ate and so on. If the person has no photographs (this is sadly more often the case), it may be possible to check whether there are any family members who would be willing and able to supply some. They may even provide information to go with them, and client, supporter and other people involved with the client can even discover and share a collaborative sense of adventure in the joint effort to enable the person with learning disabilities to find out about their past.

Drawing
If there is no access to either family or photos, it is possible to indentify the slightest fragments that the person you are supporting offers and build from there. Representational drawing can be offered by the supporter; in other words, the supporter draws what the person remembers using basic boxes and matchstick people and adds labels with all the details that are given as memories emerge. Being a great artist is not the issue here! In fact, it could even distract from the process in hand. Simple line drawings are more than adequate, and can create amusement for both parties. It is more important that the right questions are asked, questions that help both client and supporter to build up a sense of the hospital ward or the school or the family home.

Using the senses

The senses are an important key to reminiscing:

Taste	remembering particular food, who prepared and cooked it, the role that the person reminiscing played in helping to get it ready. Some food could be prepared and shared together while reminiscing
Smell	a particular perfume, a particular place
Sound	a train, the sea
Touch	sand, a woollen rug, a pet
Sight	photos from resource packs or magazines, brochures, maps, or places of significance visited and photos taken of the trip

When thinking of prompt questions, the supporter should keep all five senses in mind. Reminiscence sessions could be built on items which stimulate the senses. Sensory triggers can be a very powerful way of enabling someone to reminisce, particularly those that stimulate the sense of smell. This is a far more immediate trigger than remembering with words, and can sometimes be quite overwhelming. Items therefore need to be introduced sensitively and slowly, one at a time.

The person with learning disabilities themselves can be encouraged to become creative in their reminiscing, by being provided with different sizes of paper and a variety of mediums such as felt pens (thin and thick), oil pastels, paints and so on. The person could be asked if they would like to draw the place or person which they are remembering. They may need the supporter to help by asking a few prompt questions, for example, What was the colour of the door? The shape of the window? Were there any trees? and so on. Or they may quickly become very absorbed, and the supporter will become a witness sitting quietly nearby as they work.

Bill's life-story book

Bill had very few memories of his mother; he had not spent very much of his life living in his family home. But he had visited his mother in her home and she had visited him in the various institutions in which he had spent his life.

The few memories he had of his mother were good ones, and from these he had built a positive image of her which he held dear. As he became older (he was in his seventies) he became very concerned that he was not sure exactly where she was buried. I felt that part of this concern was that he was worried about losing her as his memories faded. So I suggested that together we built up a life-story book together. This was made up of pictures (Bill's drawings) and anecdotes (which I wrote down for him, as he found writing difficult) that he remembered about time spent with his mother. As the book grew it also expanded to include reminiscences of his school days, time spent with his brother, life in the long stay hospital and finally moving out into a hostel and eventually a flat of his own. This book became very important to Bill; he often spent a session reading through sections of it. Both making the book and reading it through later seemed to help Bill to put some perspective on his life. It also became a useful way for him to keep hold of and integrate memories of his mother into his life.

A book is not necessarily the right creative form for everyone's reminiscence. Some people are very uncomfortable about reading and writing, having been made to feel a failure during their school days. Even if they do not have to actually read or write anything in order to make a life-story book, it still may not be a medium which appeals to them. There are many other forms that creative reminiscence can take (see Resource List for further reading). Below is an account of a piece of work which I carried out with a man who was visually impaired. Naturally, a book would not have been appropriate in his case, so I chose to use clay with him.

Reminiscing with Leonard

Leonard, a man in his late sixties, had a visual impairment which meant that he could see very little, but he had adapted to coping with this very well. After a while it was easy to forget about the impairment in his presence. After the death of his mother (who was his last surviving parent) he had become very preoccupied with the fact that relatives had descended on his mother's house and emptied it of everything; he had not been given anything at all. He became fixated on a boat, which he had made out of concrete with his father when he was a small boy, and which had always lived on top of his mother's coalbunker. He was heartbroken to think that he no longer knew where it was. I was very struck by his pain over this. When he spoke about it, he seemed to become an abandoned small boy again. I felt that this memory linked him to a time in his life when his family was all together, and that it was important for him to be in touch with this feeling of connection again.

We decided together that Leonard could make a replica of the boat, so that he could show me what it was like. I provided some clay and he worked on it each session for many weeks. All the time he was working, he would talk to me about his father and his memories of the things they had done together; he talked angrily of the other relatives, and he reminisced about his mother. When the boat was finally finished, Leonard decided to paint it. He chose a fluorescent pink paint, perhaps because this colour was bright enough for him to make out the shape of the boat. At the end of our work together he took the boat home and it now lives in his bedroom. Through this creative piece of reminiscence, Leonard was able to make some good internal links to his parents. I also think that the pummeling and kneading of the clay allowed him to vent some of the frustration, impotence and anger that had been stirred in him by his relatives' behaviour.

Using and making stories

One of the functions of therapy is the 'storying' and' restorying' of lives (Tomm 1990). For some people, it is too painful to work directly with their own story; they may perhaps also feel unused to and uncomfortable with too much attention on themselves. Bowman (1994) suggests that poetry and other forms of 'bibliotherapy' (the therapeutic use of written material) are tools that can be used effectively in facilitating mourning. He describes the use of published narratives and poems in order to enable someone to reflect on or understand more fully the process they are experiencing. Myths and archetypal stories can also be used. Gersie (2003) informs us that:

> In the last two decades, professional and academic attention to the potential of stories to trigger and support difficult change processes has (also) burgeoned, as have therapeutic practices that regularly use narrative-based methods such as story making. (p. 6)

All of these resources, story-making, focusing on characters within stories and myths, or descriptions from the real experiences of other bereaved people, can provide useful methods for allowing reflection from a distanced perspective. They have the potential of highlighting experiences that mirror elements of the person's own life. Working in this way provides emotional safety. Through the structure of the story, the client is able to recognize and take from it whatever they are ready to hear and to understand in relation to themselves. The metaphorical nature of a story often makes it easier to gain insight into one's own situation, bringing with it a new slant to a previously 'stuck' way of thinking.

Stories are intrinsically linked with change; fearing change, facing up to change, and finding ways of coping with it. Stories can generate questions and curiosity and can develop flexible thinking. They are therefore a very useful way of working with people at a time of bereavement. Gersie (1991) says:

> ...therefore the wise old storytellers of yesteryear told the ancient tales about life and death, of adventure and misadventure. Stories which reconciled and those which generated more questions than they answered. (p. 37)

Below I share some of my experiences of using stories with people with learning disabilities.

Devising stories – story-making

Most traditional stories contain within them core story grammar elements. These are: a setting, one or more characters, an initiating event (the character's task, goal or mission), helpers and opponents or good fortune and misfortune, a resolution and coda (Gersie 1983, Gersie & King 1990).

I have tried devising new stories that make use of some of these story grammar elements as a way to assess someone with learning disabilities when they are finding it difficult to share very much about their own life. I might suggest to the client that we forget about their own situation for a while, and instead do some creative work. I then invite them to think of what might fit some story grammar elements, one at a time. These elements might be:

1 A main character
2 A mission or task
3 A helper
4 An obstacle
5 How the main character copes
6 An outcome (Gersie 1983, 1984, 1989, Lahad 1992)

I encourage them to draw something representative for each of these elements. When this is done, the clients are encouraged to tell the story in their own words. Gersie calls this technique question-based storymaking (Gersie 1989). I mostly used a version of Gersie's technique, mentioned by Lahad, who calls it 6-piece storymaking or 6-PSM. I also use Lahad's assessment tool (BASIC-Ph) to note the person's tone of voice and any changes that may occur in the telling of the story. I also note whether the person has engaged in imaginative thought or whether the story has remained in the realms of the everyday.

I often find that people with learning disabilities make stories that contain very little imaginative thought. The stories are often based within their own world - the world that they know. More worryingly, the client can often become 'stuck' in not being able to think of a helper or of a resolution. This of course could lead to a very vulnerable position for the client in therapy, where their perceived helplessness becomes reinforced. In the past, I have overcome these situations by making suggestions, and we have proceeded with the story together. But this tactic avoids the purpose of the client finding coping strategies within themselves. It is something that has frustrated me for a long time, and although I am often creative at finding flexible ways of adapting processes for people with learning disabilities, I felt that my thinking about this had also become 'stuck'. In other words, my countertransference response was that I felt helpless about my clients' helplessness.

Dramatherapist, author and storyteller, Alida Gersie draws on her deep experience of this work in stressing the importance of recognising that Lahad adapted the technique of question-based storymaking into 6-PSM for a particular purpose with a very particular, and basically healthy, though recently traumatised client group. She feels alarmed at the way Lahad's 6-PSM is now being used in very different contexts, with the potential for non-beneficial clinical practice.

In supervision with her, it was useful for me to reflect on how easily I had fallen into doing this, and once I had gained an understanding, I could see why this process was not working in the way that I had hoped that it would. Although I do not in any way consider that people with learning disabilities fit into a category of being unwell, I realised that I had not considered thoroughly enough the fact that many people with learning disabilities, even though mentally well, may still not be cognitively able to complete this process because of the issue of dependency intrinsic to having a disability. The stigma that society places on dependence, which can become internalized within people with learning disabilities (see Chapter 2) is highly likely to make it difficult for a client to come up with an assessment story containing positive 'helper' elements. Needing help can be considered a weakness.

I had approached Alida because I was particularly interested in talking with her about the building of 'story grammar' elements; I felt that this was an area where I and my clients were getting stuck.

Many people with learning disabilities may not have been exposed very often to the range of creative 'nourishment' that other people have, such as stories they could read or have told to them, theatre, film or music. Even where there has been wide exposure of this kind, some people with learning disabilities may not have the cognitive capacity to hold onto the range of images that they may have experienced. As Gersie puts it 'there is a need to build a cognitive emotional capacity for thinking in the narratised world' (2003 personal communication). In order to do this, the therapist needs to engage the client in building up their own Core Story Grammar Components; these are slightly different from the six components of 6-PSM already mentioned in that they also contain landscapes and dwelling places, which can help the client locate the story. The more concrete elements (such as location) can provide the stepping-stones towards some of the more abstract thoughts such as 'what is at stake?', or even inspire positive and imaginative thoughts about 'helpers'. From this 'grammar' a full story can be created, including a resolution and outcome. To repeat: the Core Story Grammar Components are as follows:

- Landscapes
- Dwelling places
- Characters (creatures or humans)
- What is at stake (problems, missions or tasks)
- Helpers

Gersie suggests a useful way to help people who have difficulty in holding different options within their thinking is to support them to develop a range of cards within the different Story Grammar Components. These cards can be drawn or painted, or images can be torn from magazines and so on, and made into collages for each of the different themes. The aim is to build up a repertoire of cards within each theme. This is likely to be a long process in itself. It does not have to occur in every session, but can be done over a period of time, dipping in and out of the creative work in between whatever else comes up in the sessions. Gersie adds that it is also useful to build up some words and/or symbols cards, and additional plain white cards that can be used to create new items within the categories as the story builds.

Once the cards are made, story-making can be used with the client drawing on his or her own 'self made' range of different worlds and characters, which the therapist has enabled them to create as cue cards. This process enriches the person with learning disabilities' creative options in story-making, and ultimately in problem-solving and coping in their own lives. It is also likely that the person with learning disabilities will begin to retain some of the images that they have been facilitated to create; this is then reinforced by the use of the images within the stories.

To address the issue of how story-making itself could be introduced to people with learning disabilities, Gersie has devised the idea of 'seed' or 'minimal' stories. 'These are stories which exist in a very minimal way' (personal communication 2003). The client is encouraged to build a sentence which contains a verb and a character, such as 'The king died'. The therapist then works with the client to expand the story, by formulating questions based around the story grammar elements or components as listed above (Question-based story-making, Gersie 2003) using the cards which have been made previously. The aim is to work with the client in supporting them to build a full story with a resolution. Supporting someone to develop their innate creativity in this way is a very positive way of building up the person's self esteem which, as stated at the beginning of this chapter, is particularly important at a time of bereavement.

The discussion above demonstrates my own use of supervision as a process that supported me to work through the helplessness that I was feeling in attempting to make stories with my clients. The transference had arrested my creativity and thinking. Although I knew that drawing would be useful for this client group rather than relying soley on words, this was not enough. Once I began to talk this through with a 'knowledgeable other', I began to understand far more about what had been happening, and with support from my supervisor, start thinking again, and find a way forward.

Creative use of archetypal (traditional) stories

On occasion I have been working with clients with learning disabilities and a particular archetypal story comes to my mind. It is evoked by the situation of the client and by my intimate knowledge of the story. Gersie (2003) suggests that it is better for a therapist to have a small repertoire of stories that are truly internalized, than a large range of vaguely remembered ones.

Such stories can be helpful to use with bereaved clients as a way of introducing a similar theme to the issue with which they are currently struggling. Whenever this has happened I introduce the idea to the client by saying, *"I have just thought of a story which you may know as well, would you like me to tell it to you?"* I then facilitate reflection on the story, which may lead to further creative work, depending on how the client takes to the story. Using a story in this way allows the client some emotional distance from their own story, while at the same time facilitating some insight into their situation. The story does not have to be overtly about death; sometimes the issue might be more to do with complex relationships. Below is an account of one such situation.

Ann and Gill

Ann was referred after the death of her father, to whom she had been very close. She had a moderate learning disability. Ann was referred because she had become increasingly aggressive towards her peers, and had isolated herself so much that she had had to move from a shared flat into a bedsit on her own within the same hostel. Gill had been referred because she had begun to wander off from the flat in which she lived and had become lost and disorientated; she was also showing signs of depression. Her social worker had recognised the wandering as 'searching' behaviour. It appeared to have been triggered by a member of staff leaving, with whom Gill had had a strong relationship. It also seemed linked to unresolved grief over her mother's death a few years earlier, and perhaps the death of her father. Gill was living alone in supported housing and was very lonely and unhappy there.

Both Ann and Gill underwent the six week assessment individually, and it was decided from this that they would each benefit from working together in a small group.

Both found it difficult to be together at first. Ann did not enjoy sharing her time with someone else, whereas Gill did not feel entitled to any attention. They had both had a similar experience of the loss of the original counsellor who had done the assessments with them, and the individual time that they had each had alone with her. This became the starting point for them to find some common ground, which gradually led to a little more sharing and the discovery of similarities and differences. Shortly into the work with me they each shared with the other the story of the death of their parents, which led to the beginnings of empathy between them. A few weeks later, they were able to share some of their feelings about the major losses they had experienced, very tentatively at first, then in a very concrete way, through voice, movement and art materials.

Some way into the therapy, the theme of bullying siblings came up as a major issue for both of them. At this point I introduced the story of Cinderella, as it contained many pertinent elements, these being: a wicked parent, a passive parent, an idealised parent, bullying siblings, internalisation of the love of the dead parent and the discovery of self worth. At first I tentatively suggested the story during a session at which only Ann was present; she had been talking of her relationship with her sisters, and I had been reminded of the story as she spoke. I asked Ann if she knew the story and she did, although she found it hard to relate. We gradually pieced the story together between us. We then enacted a scene between one of the sisters and Cinderella.

I took the part of Cinderella and Ann took the part of the sister. At first she found it very difficult to act being nasty, bullying or unfair towards me as Cinderella. This may have been because she knew how it felt to be on the receiving end, or perhaps she also feared that she would damage me in some way and that her bullying would become uncontainable, as it sometimes had with her peers in the hostel. Reflecting on this was very difficult for Ann; it was not something that she was used to doing and her attention span was brief. We then spoke about how Cinderella might have felt when her sisters were being horrible to her. This seemed easier for her to think about; she made an indirect comparison with her own situation. The session ended with Ann deciding to make a large picture of Cinderella in her ballgown. In order to get a large enough image, I suggested that either one of us could be drawn around by the other, and that this shape could then be transformed into Cinderella in the ballgown. Ann decided that she would like to be drawn around, and once this had been done, she added features to the face and drew shoes and a dress on the image.

This session felt as though it had been important; it was the first time that Ann had shared the extent of the pain she felt from her sisters' behaviour towards her. The fact that she felt trusting enough of me to lie down and be drawn around was also positive. I was pleased and moved that it was her image rather than mine that would become transformed into the princess in the ballgown. Both Ann and Gill took little pride in their appearance. There was almost a sense that they sabotaged themselves and did not allow themselves to appear their physical best, for fear, perhaps, of rejection. If they did not make an effort, then they could always fantasize that things could be different.

At the next session Gill returned, and we told her how we had been working with the story of Cinderella the week before. I felt that the issues of bullying and loss present in the story would also be resonant for Gill and had therefore thought that it would be pertinent to continue to use this story if she seemed interested. I brought in a book with the original story of Cinderella and offered to read it. This suggestion was greeted with great enthusiasm by both Ann and Gill.

Quite a lot of time was then spent discussing the bits of the story that had really stood out for each of them. Ann commented that the father should not have allowed the step-sisters to behave so horribly towards Cinderella. This was a very important reflection, and led to her reporting how her own beloved father had never tackled her sisters' treatment of her. This was the first time that Ann had been able to allow herself to think anything negative about him. I felt relieved that at last she was allowing some flexibility in her thinking about her father, as up until that point she had idealised him. It was however quite a sad realization for her, as until then Ann had never questioned her positive feelings towards her father and had not considered why he had not done anything to stop her sisters. After her initial feelings of anger and disappointment, Ann developed a much more balanced memory of him which still had many happy memories and was not so defended.

Gill focused on the importance of the mother's grave as a source of comfort for Cinderella. This led her to talk about how much she liked to visit her own mother's grave, but how this had become harder since the bus routes had changed. Ann joined in with a mixture of sadness and anger saying that she had never been to her father's grave, and did not even know where he was buried. I supported both women in discussing these difficulties with their escorts after the session, in order that some practical steps could be taken to support them in visiting the graves as and when they wanted to. This is a demonstration of the importance of working closely with the person and their support network. At roc, from the start of a piece of therapeutic work with an individual, we establish that we include the support system. This enables the therapeutic work to be backed up by practical action wherever necessary and opens the way for collaboration and guidance.

The work continued, using this story as a catalyst for several weeks. Each session began with a reading of the original story; a deepening reflection on the themes unfolded. During some sessions short improvisations took place, which led to further discussions, and each session ended with some time working on the collage of Cinderella in her gown. The original story ends with Cinderella finding happiness and love, symbolised by her transformation from wearing rags to becoming a princess in a ballgown, a transformation from not being valued to being valued. The large picture of Cinderella that Ann had begun became a shared collage representing this transformation. It took them many sessions to complete, and the informal talking and sharing that took place as it was being created was important in nurturing their understanding and support of one another. It became a symbol of their growing relationship with each other. This friendship was also beginning to take place outside the sessions (they had met for lunch once, and another time had tea together). This was an important development for Ann and Gill, given that loneliness and isolation had been a major difficulty for each of them at the start of this intervention.

The use of rituals

Rituals have been defined in a variety of forms. (Haviland 1978, Chapple 1970). Douglas talks of 'the relation between both individual psychological needs and public social needs, both expressed by symbolic acts' (1975 p. 61). These may be events designed to make a crisis less socially disruptive, and at the same time, more 'containing' for the individuals most closely affected. They may include celebration and symbolism, and can serve to facilitate expressions of collective emotion.

Within all cultures and religions, rituals take place when a member of that community dies. This ritual serves to mark various transitions. These will vary from culture to culture and from belief system to belief system. For example, these may include the transition from a relationship with the deceased in life through to a continued but changed relationship with the deceased in death, and the beginning of the spiritual journey of the deceased on to another life.

Every funeral is different. Some religions and cultures prescribe precise rituals and customs within which there may be particular roles for individual members of the family. Others are less structured, and may allow for friends and family to make the ceremony individual and tailored to the specific needs of the chief mourners. Within some cultures and religions it is common to have an open casket and for people to view the body of the deceased, whereas in others, this would be taboo. Some traditions direct whether the body is buried or cremated, whilst in other cultures it is a personal choice for the family concerned. Many people experience a sense of the customs and constructs which traditionally surrounded death in our society breaking down. Rituals may be less pre-scribed, and although this can provide a freedom for people to express their grief in more personal ways (which can be positive), it can also leave others feeling slightly at sea at a difficult time.

As has already been described, many people with learning disabilities are not included in funerals; this is often upsetting and unhelpful for the person in enabling them to grieve healthily. I have demonstrated exam-ples of the benefits of retrospective memorials devised with the client and supported by a spiritual leader, as in the stories of Philip and Alan in Chapters 6 and 9. However, sometimes there is a need for something further, perhaps in order to mark an anniversary or to come to terms with a particularly difficult experience, such as abuse or rape. A ritual can provide a link to the person with whom an actual dialogue can no longer be had; it can provide a space within which a profound goodbye can be given form, and it can enable a different internalized relationship to begin with the deceased.

All the rituals that I have supported people to devise within therapy have been completely individual. For some, they were rehearsals for what would eventually become a memorial held in a church or other place of worship. For others, the work with me in the session was enough in itself. Some clients have brought elements of their own particular belief system to the rituals, where for others, it has been purely secular.

I provide a number of key materials. I offer candles (important in many religious and spiritual practices, and themselves holding numerous symbolic meanings); musical instruments, flowers, feathers, silks, recorded music and art materials. I support the person to devise something that they would like to say. I also offer my services to read or to say anything that they would like me to, and we sometimes sing. It usually takes several sessions to devise the ritual; when it takes place it is carried out with reverence.

Sometimes the ritual simply consists of devising a letter or a script (more often than not I scribe for the person, in other words, I write down what they would like to say). This is not a letter that will ever be sent (they are often to the deceased), but it is a chance to re-frame experiences and feelings, to examine regrets and to try to draw something positive from these which can be incorporated into the person's life now. The person may then be supported in thinking what they would like to happen to the document next. They may like to light a bonfire and burn it, they may want to tear the paper into tiny pieces and scatter them in a particular place, they may want to take it to the grave itself, or they may want to keep it.

One woman I have worked with decided she would like to have what she had written published, so that other people could learn from her experience and might not have to go through anything similar. I supported her to make this happen. Her account was published in the journal *Community Living* (2002).

This is what she wrote:

I have a learning disability. I live in my own flat. When I was 16 years old and still living with my family a mishap took place. I was visiting my best friend's house as I often did. I was talking to her about her mum. Then her older brother came in. He had a learning disability as well. I was cleaning windows with my friend and her brother asked me if I wanted to see something in his room. I went with him and he asked me to sit on the bed and showed me a picture, then he kissed me and then I was amazed to find he was trying to have sex with me and before I knew it he had raped me. I didn't know what was happening. I was a bit confused. I was very upset and ran all the way home crying. My mum said, "What on earth is the matter with you?" I couldn't tell her - I felt frightened.

Then the evening came and eventually I told her. I felt really dirty. She took me down to the police station. I had to talk to a policeman and a policewoman. They asked me if I knew what a penis looked like and if I could draw what I thought it was like. After I had spoken to them the policeman spoke to my mother; he asked her if she wanted to press charges. Mum said "No". Then I was looked at by a man doctor, I had a blood test taken and then the doctor looked at my private parts. I felt angry with the doctor, I hoped it would be a lady doctor. I felt disgusted having a man touch me again. Then I was taken home. Then the next day my clothes and underwear were brought back from the police station.

I couldn't handle talking to everyone about it and nobody talked to me about it. As the weeks went by it got a little better and a little better.

I feel now that women who have been raped must say what has happened to them, they mustn't bottle it up, because otherwise it eats you up inside and makes you angry.

It wasn't until about a year afterwards that I was able to talk about it. My mum and I were sitting down together and she began, she said I needed to put it to the back of my mind and get on with my life.

In that year I became angry and upset. I was upset with my mum and I was angry with him. I couldn't let any men touch me, not even my dad. I felt so afraid it was awful.

I have coped all these years by putting it to the back of my mind. But it has always affected my relationships with men, sometimes the anger crawls in again, particularly when I hear in the news of women or children who have been raped – I become filled up with anger inside.

After my mum died I started feeling that I wanted to die and be with her. I also began to feel very angry with my mum because I felt that when she was alive we never really dealt with the rape properly. We didn't try to prosecute him and that began to take over my thoughts more and more.

I know that women have the right to say 'No' and I would like all women to know that.

It was a very positive experience for this woman to have her writing published; it validated her experience and helped to undo some of the hurt caused by having to remain silent for so long. This in turn enabled her to forgive her deceased mother and helped her in her ability to grieve.

In this chapter, I have highlighted the importance of a thorough assessment of the individual's situation after bereavement in order that the best support at various levels, social, spiritual and emotional, can be put in place. I have emphasised the importance of not only focusing on grief, but also considering empowering the bereaved individual in order that they can develop new skills or build on existing ones and nurture their creative selves. I have also suggested a number of ways in which the bond between the bereaved and the deceased can be sustained.

Chapter 8

Encouraging communication about the unspeakable

People with learning disabilities are often given very confusing information on difficult and complicated life themes such as death, sex and their own dependence. They may indeed be given none at all, and are left in the dark trying to make sense of their experiences. Hollins and Grimer (1988) identify these life themes as the 'three secrets'. Gersie (1991) reminds us:

> Silence on death issues leaves us vulnerable to manipulation, as well as frightened and impoverished. True awareness of death generates the motivation to bring about change. (p. 37)

Encouraging communication is a positive way of breaking the conspiracy of silence that so often surrounds people with learning disabilities.

The previous two chapters explored the use of therapy and counselling. This brief chapter continues in a similar vein by thinking specifically about the benefits and difficulties connected to running groups with clients with learning disabilities. Groups can encourage people to share experience, listen to each other, learn and be curious. I will examine two different models: death education, and bereavement therapy groups.

Bicknell (1983) describes how it is often as a result of a 'life event', such as bereavement, that insight is triggered. It is on this premise that I would advocate interventions that facilitate exploration, reflection, support and communication when someone with a learning disability is facing the death of someone close to them. Such an intervention might be pre-emptive and proactive, before the death of the significant person. Here, *death education groups* are very useful. As a response to the impact of a prior bereavement, a discussion/support group or a *bereavement therapy group* would be appropriate, which could explore issues on a deeper level.

There are many challenges involved in running groups with people with learning disabilities. Some of these are practical; transport, location, ensuring that people have support such as escorts if needed. Facilitators must also find the appropriate level at which to pitch communication for the whole group, establish a pace which suits all the participants, and find ways to deal with (unconscious) attacks on thinking (described previously and see below). Such attacks challenge group facilitators to address their countertransference responses (see Chapter 6) and find ways to overcome the difficulty in establishing a sense of flow or cohesiveness in the sessions. The role of supervision is crucial, in that it provides an essential space for group facilitators to unravel their responses in relation to the issues being addressed by the group

Death education groups

It has been reported repeatedly that people with learning disabilities often lack knowledge and life experience that others take for granted, and which can be so helpful at a time of bereavement (Persaud & Persaud 1997). To counteract this difficulty, it would be useful to think of pro-actively setting up life-cycle/death education groups for people with learning disabilities in preparation for the experience of being bereaved, or as a place within which to share feelings and experiences (Kloeppel & Hollins 1989, Oswin 1991, Read 1996). These groups would be aimed at people with mild to moderate learning disability. They could be set up as an ordinary part of people's general education within a school or college or within day services. Alternatively, they could be established specifically in anticipation of death before it occurs, for example for people with elderly parents or who have parents who are terminally ill.

Educators, day-centre workers, social workers, counsellors, therapists or skilled volunteers could facilitate the groups. What matters most is that they are run by people with an interest who have had some choice in the matter, and that some thought is also given to the support that the facilitators in turn receive. Such support may be in the form of clinical supervision and/or access to counselling support. Groups should be kept small, eight or less people. The Persauds (1997) suggest that this is an optimum number for encouraging sensitive group discussion, and is also a reasonable number of people to manage in a practical sense if field trips are to be undertaken. The aim of these groups should be to provide some or all of the following:

1 A discussion forum for issues of general loss
2 Some basic information about the life cycle
3 Some discussion about feelings - their identification and expression
4 Information about the components of the concept of death
5 Basic information about bereavement and how people cope with loss
6 Field trips to chapels of rest, funeral parlours, cemeteries, crematoriums and graveyards

These groups should be held over an extended period of time rather than an intensive week, as this gives the individuals a chance to internalise and personalise the content (Yanok & Beifus 1993).

It is important to assess people before they take part in a group of this sort, in order that the facilitator has a good knowledge of each individual, their abilities and their needs. The assessments should ascertain an individual's experience of death. This could include whether the person has experienced a death, how long ago this was, and what effect talking about it has on them now. Similarly, if someone close to the person is likely to die soon, it will be important to clarify the person's understanding and whether they are able to talk about this. It would also be useful to try to find out something about their concept of death, and whether the person can read and/or write.

Once people have been identified for a potential group, they should be given accessible information about the content of the course. It is important that people are able to make an informed choice as to whether they wish to take part or not. Some people may not be able to do this until they begin to take part in the group. It is therefore useful to ensure that people can safely leave the group if they need to and are never forced to take part.

Bereavement therapy groups
Group therapy with people with learning disabilities has been documented previously in a small but detailed literature (Hollins & Evered 1990,

Gravestock & McGauley 1994, Pantlin 1985, Hollins & Sinason 2000), which highlights the likelihood of the themes of dependency, handicap, and sexuality arising.

Ideally, facilitators aim to bring together a 'compatible group' of people with similar issues, similar cognitive abilities, with a gender balance and with a consideration of an appropriate mix of ages. In my experience, however, it is rarely possible to form the ideal group. People's needs, and the pressure of a waiting list means that within our service, we often have to take a chance when we form a group, and hope that it will gel. Some groups work better than others, but we learn something new about the process each time.

Simpson (2002) stresses the importance of psychological and psychiatric assessments for clients before the onset of therapy. He suggests that this may help to determine the level of organic impairment and to establish when there is a psychiatric condition or a 'secondary handicap' that could make the person appear more disabled than they are. I am uncertain, however, whether tests can do this, or whether they simply indicate the individual's level of functioning. A low level of functioning could be because of secondary handicap or because of regression in connection to grief. It would be impossible to know which until the therapy was underway. However, if there is a possibility that a client referred for therapy might be showing signs of dementia, then screening can be invaluable, as dementia and depression can often be mistaken for one another. Referrals for dementia assessments can be made to the community team for people with learning disabilities (psychology department).

Ultimately, in my experience, it is not always possible to determine just who will gain from the therapy before the process begins. My sense is that it is not until the process has started that it is possible to see the client's capacity to think and their true intelligence emerge. It is suggested that within the first year of psychotherapy, there is a marked decrease in secondary handicap.

However, Simpson (2002) warns that there is a tendency for therapists to fall into a defensive trap. He describes how the label 'learning disability' can become a 'refuge from knowledge' for everyone around the learning disabled person; this can work as a two-way process. It can either manifest as an over-estimation of the ability of the person and unwillingness to know the limitations of the organic impairment, or as an under-estimation of the person's ability and an unwillingness to recognize that there may also be some psychological disturbance. He suggests that as therapists, we are more likely to hold onto the former in the hope that the person may perhaps have a secondary handicap that is making them appear more disabled than they actually are. My feeling is that I would rather give someone the benefit of the doubt and work as if there is likely to be a secondary handicap. If, after a period of therapeutic assessment, there is little change, I would then refer them on for a psychiatric and/or psychological assessment. In this way we would not be excluding anyone or making pre-judgments before beginning work.

With this in mind, when setting up a therapeutic group, it would be good practice to structure the first month or two of the group as a therapeutic assessment. This provides a chance for the individuals to get know something of what they are agreeing to take part in. At the end of this time, group members would then be able to make an informed decision as to whether they would like to make a commitment to the group. The therapists will know if they feel that there is a need to refer an individual for further or more formal assessment, or if anyone is perhaps not suited to group work.

Benefits of group work
One of the main benefits of working in a death education or bereavement therapy group is that curiosity about the subject and about each other's experiences can be encouraged. People with learning disabilities are often expected to be passive and not to ask questions; this can limit their experience of life. It is through being inquisitive that we learn and grow. In order to have more choices and options available to us, we need to be interested in what life has to offer. This includes being interested in difficult issues such as death.

Stokes and Sinason (1992) distinguish between emotional and cognitive intelligence. They state that people with learning disabilities often have emotional intelligence, and they describe what they see as the handicapped and the non-handicapped parts of the personality. They recognize that just because someone has a learning disability, it does not mean that there are not parts of that person that could use psychotherapy. In his brief work with a group of people with learning disabilities, Pantlin (1985) concluded that groups could encourage emotional development. Rudnitzki (1988), who worked with a group of young people with a range of disabilities, suggested that the group could act as a 'psychosocial prosthesis', enabling group members to explore, share and accept their individual assets and disabilities. Hollins and Evered (1990) report on a group which they ran which consisted of seven members of both genders all with IQs between fifty-two and seventy-eight. They describe how despite many conflicts persisting, the participants had become more reflective by the end of the group. They state that it appears to have been a positive experience for group members. Other gains they describe are the liberation of creative energy, the relief of emotional pain through cathartic expression, talking about painful issues such as not being wanted and some curiosity and interest in other group members.

My colleague David O'Driscoll and I regularly run bereavement therapy groups. Amongst other things, we encourage individuals to offer their advice and experience to other members of the group. This has proved rewarding and valuable for all group members. The role of helper can be empowering and can enable a person's self-confidence and self-esteem to grow. It also lessens the group members' dependence on us as facilitators or as 'the ones with knowledge', to come up with answers. It also encourages more initiative and less passivity, and awakens participants' awareness that the group members hold quite a lot of knowledge between themselves.

I have often found that it seems difficult for people with learning disabilities to listen to and to take an interest in each other, and to remember important things about other people. This is perhaps linked to the devaluing of peers that has been mentioned elsewhere in this book, resulting from society's devaluing of people with learning disabilities. It may also be linked to cognitive and social development. The individual may not have reached the developmental stage of being less preoccupied with the self and of developing an interest in others. The group therapists can encourage this development.

Model of self-help

Many people who have experienced bereavement decide to use their experience to help others. This may be a part of their resolution process. As Klass et al (1996) state:

> Helping others is one of the ways to find new meaning for the pain they have experienced, and a way to express the meaning of the transformed bonds with their loved ones.   (p. 354)

Hence we see organizations such as *Compassionate Friends, Widow to Widow* programmes and so on (see Resource List). People with learning disabilities rarely get the chance to put themselves in the place of helper, although this is often a role which some people will take on with great dedication, given the opportunity.

An organization in Newcastle (UK) called Skills for People *has taken up this idea. The work of this group is driven by the ideas and skills of self-advocates (adults living locally who have learning disabilities).* Skills for People *provides training and run groups. It has been interested in the field of bereavement for several years, and held a conference for people with learning disabilities on this subject in 2001.*

One of the self advocates, David Knight, held a workshop at the conference, and decided that his next step would be to train in counselling skills, in order to be able to provide support for others. Skills for People *worked with a counsellor in order to help members develop listening skills. They then piloted a peer-listening service, for people with a learning disability who had experienced bereavement. The pilot highlighted certain difficulties; the organization learned that listening in this way is a real skill, which they did not feel they had adequately developed. As David Knight says, 'They were glad that they had given it a try' and it is something which may be given more thought in the future.*

In the meantime Skills for People *now offers a four-day training programme on loss and bereavement aimed at people with learning disabilities. It has been designed by and is run by the self advocates. It covers the subjects of feelings, funerals, wills, poetry, coping strategies, supporting each other and sharing experiences. This course is run regularly and proves very popular. The group also recognizes that there is still a need for a one-to-one-service. Some of the self-advocates have been working with local Cruse Bereavement Counsellors in order to extend the counsellors' skills and knowledge about learning disability. This has enabled the service to offer a more appropriate and sensitive service to bereaved people with learning disabilities in the area.*

This is a very positive example of how, when motivated people with learning disabilities are given access to information, training and support, good things can happen.

Chapter 9

Will anyone care when I die?

There is a stigma attached to disability. Other chapters have examined the fear that is unconsciously evoked by disability in the non-disabled population. The consequences of this stigma often lead to rejection and exclusion. This chapter examines some of the forms this may take, and also considers the impact the consciousness of our own mortality has on the lives we live, with specific focus on how this may affect someone with a learning disability.

The knowledge of our mortality is often held as a secret. We hardly dare think of it ourselves, and we do not speak of it to others. This innate secrecy, born of fear, makes it difficult for certain sections of society to make sense of mortality and death. This is particularly true of children and people with learning disabilities, who are both often excluded from conversations, rituals and plans surrounding this taboo subject. For many of us, however, the positive side of thinking about our own death is that it enables us to reflect upon our life in the present. It is through the relationships that we make and the impact we have on the world that we will be remembered. Daring to think about death enables us to consider and revise our choices.

For many people with learning disabilities, this benefit may be undermined by an overwhelming sense of sadness that they have not been able to follow their choices, or to live a fulfilled life. There are likely to be many important things that they have not been able to do. These may range from the profound experiences of love, marriage and parenthood, to simply being able to choose where and how they would like to live or whether they have a job. Above all there may be a struggle with the question that opens this chapter, *"Will anyone care when I die?"*

Social exclusion

I recently attended a residential creative activity week. There were a lot of people on the course, there was a wide age range, and the participants came from all sorts of backgrounds and professions. Amongst them was a mother with a daughter who has Down syndrome. I was often aware that the daughter, when not with her mother, spent much of the time sitting on her own or near others, but not taking part in their conversation. People often acknowledged her and maybe asked one or two questions about her day, but this interest quickly fizzled out and people moved on to being with the new friends they had been making throughout the week.

Part-way through the week, we were all invited to an evening of entertainment. On my arrival, the young woman and I greeted each other and she asked if I would like to sit next to her. I explained that my friend had come ahead of me and had already reserved a seat for me, and I then moved off to take my seat. As the evening wore on, I became acutely aware of this woman's isolation as no-one sat with her; people sat next to her, but they were always with someone else and seemed hardly to notice her. This troubled me throughout the performance. At the end of the event I went up to say goodnight to her, and we chatted a little about the show we had just seen. I then suggested that as I had not been able to sit with her, we could perhaps have lunch together the next day; she gave me a big smile and said that would be a good idea.

The next day we met and sat together at a table full of other course participants. We chatted easily for the first ten minutes or so and then gradually other people around the table also began to engage me in conversation. To begin with I was still conscious to keep my lunch companion involved, but before I knew it, I had become engaged in a very focussed conversation with one of the other diners, and my companion had been left behind. I eventually became aware of what had happened and turned back to her to re-engage. By this time she had almost completely turned away from me, and was complaining that she wasn't sitting close enough to her mum and that her mum was busy talking to someone else.

From that point on it was very difficult to get a conversation going again. I felt terrible; I had let her down just as everyone always did. I had not facilitated the speed or the level of the conversation so that she could remain involved. It was just too easy to forget and to exclude her, even though my intention had been different. She, however, knew that the one person, the only person who would not forget her, would be her mother.

The above is just one everyday example of how people with learning disabilities are excluded from even the most ordinary of activities.

In describing social isolation and the subsequent psychic isolation disabled people experience, John McDermot (1986) emphasises that it is the emotional experience of disability that is often not considered. The oppression and exclusion experienced in the external world become internalised and form a cycle, which can be hard to break. Mason says:

> Once oppression has been internalised, little force is needed to keep us submissive. We harbour inside ourselves the pain and the memories, the fears and the confusions, the negative self images and the low expectations, turning them into weapons with which to re-injure ourselves, every day of our lives.
>
> (Mason 1992, p. 27)

This is similar to Sinason's (1992) theory of 'opportunist handicap', mentioned earlier. In the experience I have just described, this woman had learned that she would be left out, so she isolated herself in preparation by withdrawing from the conversation. On an unconscious level, I allowed it to happen by not slowing the conversation down, thus fulfilling her expectation of me. Todd (2002) describes this psychic isolation as social death.

When it comes to important life events exclusion becomes more overt. For example, as I have described in Chapter 5, it is still rare for people with learning disabilities to get married, and someone with a learning disability is more likely to become an aunt or uncle than a parent themselves. It is almost as though they are cast in the role of onlookers to other people's lives, and when it comes to the rituals that surround death, they are often not given a place at all. Research (Hollins 1998) has shown that fewer than one in six adults with learning disabilities who had lost a parent had visited their dying parent in hospital, and only half attended the funeral. This may often happen because the natural instinct of parents and carers is to protect their relative or client from the pain of the loss. It may also be because there is a fear that the person will become unmanageable or will not conform to 'expected' behaviour at the funeral (perhaps laughing or talking loudly at inappropriate moments). Or it may even be that the person is perceived not to understand what has happened, and therefore that 'they do not need to come'. Whatever the reason, for someone who has been excluded, the grieving process is more likely to become problematic, as has been discussed in previous chapters.

By being excluded, the person will not have the visible cues of the funeral to help make what has happened (ie the death of their relative) more real for them. They will not have the chance to see other people grieve, and will therefore not receive the message that it is normal to feel sad or angry at such a time. Many people with learning disabilities have difficulty understanding and recognising their own feelings and emotions; to be amidst other people who are experiencing acute emotions is important for them. Yet so often, just as with children, other people will hide how they are feeling in front of someone with a learning disability, because they fear that the person will not be able to cope. By being excluded, they may also miss some of the important healing processes that can happen when family and friends get together during the aftermath of a funeral, a time when people often reminisce and reflect on the deceased person's life, as well as finding ways to cope with the rest of their own lives.

Many bereaved people report that planning and organising the funeral of their loved one gave them focus and purpose during the trauma and shock immediately following a death. This process can provide a structure at a time when everything else feels chaotic. Organising a funeral can keep a family so busy that there is very little time to think or feel, which can be a welcome retreat from harsh reality. Yet rarely does the bereaved member of the family with a learning disability share this process, even if they are lucky enough to attend the funeral.

George is a man in his early seventies. He is always smartly dressed and is a polite and gentle person. He is keen to tell you that he likes to make the best of everything and get on and do things, but he often looks sad. He is the youngest child from a sibship of eight. He lived with his family until adolescence and then moved into a residential hospital. His parents both died within the same year nearly twenty years ago, and more recently, two of his sisters also died. He did not attend any of the funerals; in fact he has never been to a funeral.

On meeting George, he will very quickly tell you that both his parents and two of his sisters have died. He will tell you about his parents' deaths as though they happened yesterday. Soon after this he will say that he didn't go to the funerals, that his sisters didn't tell him about them and that they left him out; it will be clear as he tells you that this exclusion is still very painful to him. The pain of being left out seems to have almost exceeded the pain of losing his parents; he has been denied the right to say goodbye to them. The hurt that this has caused him has interrupted his life. It is very difficult for him to talk of anything else, and yet this happened to him almost twenty years ago.

It seems clear that this exclusion also takes him back to the time when he was excluded from the family home by being sent to live in a hospital. It is harder for him to talk about this. Perhaps if he allows himself to think of what happened, he may have some angry feelings towards his parents. Perhaps it feels safer for him to be angry with his brothers and sisters, who left him out and who continue to leave him out by having family get-togethers to which they do not invite him. George is a very able man, but the pain of being excluded has disabled him; his preoccupation with being left out makes it very difficult for him to focus on anything else.

The taboo of death

The biggest fear of any living conscious being is the fear of death. It is a powerful force which drives us throughout our lives. Freud (1915) wrote that 'death was the necessary outcome of life'(in Judd 1989, p. 17) but he went on to say that we have 'an unmistakable tendency to put death on one side, to eliminate it from life.' (1915 p. 289). Judd (1989) considers that the development of our negotiation with death begins in childhood. She states that:

> ... the young infant registers the possibility of death through a sense of the danger of death. It is a common observation that newborn babies cry if hungry or cold, or if they feel unsafe, as a way of signalling for help and avoiding death.   (p. 18)

Adults, however, especially in the western world, build strong psychological defences around the fear of death. There are conflicting theories as to whether this fear is innate or stems more from environmental factors. Winnicott (1954) writes ' Death, for an infant at the beginning (of life), means something quite definite, namely loss of 'being' on account of prolonged reaction to environmental impingement' (p. 134). Bowlby (1960) has described the reaction of young children to the prolonged separation from their mother as grief and mourning. He states that the young child cannot distinguish between a temporary absence and a permanent loss. The child therefore *feels as though* the mother is dead; without her presence, the child fears its own demise.

In contrast to these environmentalist views, Judd (1989) describes Klein's explanation that the fear of death arises out of the infant's paranoid fear of being killed by its own projected aggression. In other words, the infant feels anxiety from experiences such as birth, being hungry, in pain and so on, as well as receiving life-giving experiences, such as feeding and physical comfort, from its mother. When the infant is faced with anxiety-inducing experiences, she deflects the feelings or 'projects' them onto someone or something else, because at present the ego is too immature to cope. So, for example, when an infant's mother leaves the room, the infant feels frightened by the force of her anger at this, and on the return of the mother, perceives her anger not to be her own, but her mother's. The infant then becomes fearful that this angry mother will do her harm. This is thus an externalisation of the fear of death, which becomes a fear of being killed. Judd (1989) summarises by saying:

> In both views, however, it seems that the baby is forced to come up against the feeling that no good experience can last forever, and that this then leads to a need to negotiate a fear of something else - whether we call it a sense of fear of death, or anni-hilation, or disintegration, or a state of 'not-being', or, simply, of not feeling safe.   (p. 19)

As we grow older there are many changes that we negotiate along the way, each change brings with it loss and a certain amount of fear. For example, as we learn to walk so we are less carried around by our parents and we lose some of the physical closeness we once had. Death is the final transition that we face, and one which, if we face up to it and live our lives with this knowledge, can determine how we live. If we are not exposed directly to death at a young age, we learn about death gradually, taking in what we are ready to understand at different points in our development. However, acquisition of knowledge may not always be so straightforward for someone with a learning disability, as has been described elsewhere in the book (see Chapter 3).

An indication that the struggle to come to terms with mortality is present even in adulthood can be found in the terminology used to refer to death. It is common to hear euphemisms used when death is referred to, phrases such as 'passed on' or 'not with us any more'. It is as though we need to protect ourselves from the overwhelming fear of death by being indirect with the language associated with it. Perhaps there is a sense that we will not be touched by death if we do not speak its name out loud. This evasive use of language adds to the confusion and lack of knowledge for people with learning disabilities. It is important that anyone discussing death with someone with a learning disability uses direct, straightforward language, in order to be sure that people have clearly understood what is being discussed.

I was once involved in a drama workshop with people with learning disabilities; we were imagining that we were going on a space voyage. One man with quite severe learning disabilities suddenly became rather excited, as we reached the stage in the session where we were going to board the space ship. This entailed going from one room into another, and as we got to the door of the 'space rocket' he became anxious. Eventually we were able to ascertain that he thought he was going to see his father who had died; he thought he could take the rocket to heaven and meet up with his dad, who he had been told was there. Naturally, we had to disappoint him. This made me painfully aware of the concrete thinking of many people with learning disabilities, and highlights the importance of keeping explanations as straightforward and down to earth as possible.

How will I be remembered?

If we allow ourselves to consider our own death we may begin to think about how others will remember us. Will we indeed be remembered? What will be the things that people remember about us? And how will our absence affect those left behind? This thought is often brought into consciousness when we experience the death of someone close to us.

When someone with a learning disability is faced with their own mortality, particularly painful issues relating to the life that they are living may arise. As has been mentioned, many people with learning disabilities experience a great deal of loneliness (Atkinson 1989, Flynn 1989, Firth & Rapley 1990, Chappell 1994, Robertson et al 2001). They may be lucky enough to have a close and supportive family, they may have active social lives, but even with this positive scenario they are unlikely to have many or any close friends and less likely still to have a meaningful loving heterosexual or homosexual relationship. The UK Government White Paper (2001) on learning disability highlights this as an area of concern.

> People with learning disabilities are often socially isolated. Helping people sustain friendships is consistently shown as being one of the greatest challenges faced by learning disability services.
>
> (UK Department of Health White Paper 2001, p. 81)

In their paper on friendship, Pettingell and Hart (2001) describe the adults with learning disabilities they know as having very scant social lives. They write:

> Even those who are engaged in activities within a day centre, at adult education classes or attending social and leisure clubs do not seem to develop friendships or relationships that extend beyond a particular setting.'   (p. 341)

My experience is the same. I have particularly noticed that there is often reluctance among the people that I know who have a learning disability to have friendships with other people with learning disabilities (and see Chapter 5). It seems that they would rather consider professionals working with them as their friends. Pettingell and Hart (2001) also describe this phenomenon and go on to suggest that the answer may lie in society's inability to value disability:

> ... a message so strong that many people with learning disability seem themselves unable to value relationships with their peers and seek to deny their common histories.   (p. 343)

Too often the friendships and relationships made with people through other family members are disregarded once someone leaves the family and enters a residential service setting. This problem is compounded by the fact that since people are living longer, the likelihood is that there will be many older people with learning disabilities leaving the family home for the first time when a parent dies, with the result that many more people will be suddenly cut adrift from any sort of social network which they had built up around the family home.

Jung (1968) described adult development as having two specific stages. The first, childhood and youth, during which time an individual is dealing more with the outer world; and the second, in later life, where the focus shifts from the outer world to the inner world. At this time, we are more likely to contemplate our own mortality, which may lead to the thought *"Will anyone care when I die?"* Many people hope that the lives they have lived will have been worthwhile in some way, and that they will have made some sort of difference to the world. Yet many people with learning disabilities lead (by their own admission) very unproductive lives. Ashman et al (1995) interviewed people with learning disabilities who were over the age of fifty-five. Many of the interviewees had wanted to work or still wanted to, but the majority had never had the opportunity. They had often been subjected to discrimination when it came to trying to find work, even when they were perfectly capable of carrying out the tasks concerned. They also came up against all sorts of complications connected to receiving financial benefits from the state, which made the process of being in paid employment even more difficult.

Susan has a job for four hours a week cleaning in an office which she really enjoys and is good at. She has been offered another two hours work a week but cannot take it because if she were to earn over the amount she currently receives, she would lose her disability benefit. The benefit currently pays for her housing and contributes towards her bills. She also benefits from cheaper travel as someone who is registered disabled. The system is very rigid. Susan could not manage to bring in enough money a week to cover everything that her benefits do but would like to contribute more herself. There is no room for a sliding adjustment as her earnings increase.

This rigidity contributes towards the lack of job opportunities, as there are very few jobs which offer so few hours' work. It also restricts the possibility of people being able to gradually acquire skills that would enable them to build up to managing a full time job. The experience of Ashman's interviewees was, sadly, quite typical of many people with learning disabilities and the situation has changed little since this research was carried out. The reality for most people is that they will spend much of their lives in a day centre or college or gaining work experience, but not actually making a meaningful contribution to the society in which they live. This is often not at all what individuals would choose for themselves. It can contribute to a sense of worthlessness and low self-esteem, and in the context of mortality, a sense that there would be very little significance connected to one's own death.

Todd (2002) writes:

> The potential for the pre-mortem disintegration of personhood and the acute withdrawal from social interaction which dying poses can be seen as essential dimensions of the lives of people with intellectual disability some years before their deaths.
>
> (p. 228)

People who have lived for many years in long stay hospitals may have experienced little in the way of a funeral on the death of fellow patients. They may well have witnessed people being buried in unmarked graves. This will have reinforced the perception of themselves as also being not worth remembering, or deserving of tribute.

Alan is in his late sixties. He lived in institutions all his life up until 1970, and he now lives independently in a flat with minimal support. His community nurse referred him to the Loss and Bereavement service because he had a morbid preoccupation with funerals, and a huge anxiety about the expense that his own funeral would incur. He talked a lot about his mother's death and often said that he wanted to be buried beside her. At the point of referral, he had never attended a funeral. His brother had died not long before, but Alan's sister-in-law had not allowed him to go to the funeral.

Alan is verbal and has a moderate learning disability. When he is anxious or emotional, his voice becomes very loud and he fixates on issues (often from the media) that arouse fear or anger for him, and talks about them very forcefully and repetitively. During our initial meeting, the force of Alan's ranting conveyed a sense of urgency and also a sense of anger. His dialogue contained two metaphors for feeling out of control; one was dogs and the other, money. He spoke about how worried he felt that his sister-in-law had been burdened with some dogs recently; he described them as being unruly and making a lot of mess. He linked this back to his stepfather, who also kept many dogs, which caused frequent problems with neighbours. He interspersed this account with anxiety over the expense of funerals, and his concern about trying to organize payment for his own funeral costs now. Alan linked this to his concerns over his sister-in-law being left with a big bill to pay after his brother's death.

The nurse had told me before I met Alan that he was often very anxious, and that at such times his behaviour could become quite bizarre. He would become disorientated and obsessive about seeking out the most senior person in the vicinity to sort out problems for him. For example, when he received a letter from his bank which worried him, he had left his house partly shaved and not fully dressed and headed for the local Social Services office demanding to see the head of Social Services.

As we began the assessment, I was still struck by the force of anger and urgency in the way in which Alan spoke. A strong theme emerged of being remembered and valued, expressed in his concern over his mother's unmarked grave (I was later to discover that most of his experience of people dying when he lived in hospital was that they were buried in unmarked graves). Alan worried about his own grave being marked, and whether it would be remembered and tended by other people.

Over time, being 'safe' arose as another theme. This was expressed by Alan arriving at our weekly sessions on some occasions with great concerns over the safety of his cooker or his washing machine. At other times, he would focus on things in the room, which he felt were unsafe, such as a cover not being on a light or a screw missing from a chair. I wondered whether this might also have a connection to Alan feeling that he was often not in control over his own life.

During the assessment, it had become clear that there was unfinished business regarding his mother's death (he had not attended her funeral). His concept of death was in place but he was preoccupied by her death, which had occurred several years previously. It seemed that he was stuck, repeatedly going over and over his concerns about where his mother had been buried; he was not sure that she had been given a good enough funeral as he had not been there. It was difficult for him to focus on anything else. The key factors seemed to be:

1 *Not having attended the funeral*
2 *The quality of relationship he had with his mother in the first place*
3 *Feeling powerless in the situations surrounding both his mother's and his brother's deaths*
4 *Feeling that his mother would not be remembered because no-one was sure of the exact spot where she was buried and that the same fate might await him*

It also emerged that Alan felt in need of very practical information regarding funerals, having not attended that of either his brother or mother. He had a covert curiosity as to what he had missed. The specific aims set for our work together were as follows:

- *To provide some practical information regarding funerals*
- *To enable Alan to say goodbye to his mother*
- *To enable Alan to take more control in his life, for example, in terms of decision-making and friendships*

As I write about my work with Alan, it is clear that one of the aims I pursued with him was to help him to know that he really would be remembered after his death. This only became apparent to me as a need quite some way into the work, particularly as we explored his early life. Alan had been born in a home for destitute mothers and babies, and had moved around from institution to institution from birth onwards.

At one point in our work together we focused on the relationship he had with his mother. This was mainly achieved through compiling a book of his life story, and stopping from time to time to consider particular memories of his mother. These were very fragmented as he had spent very little time with her, but he held her strongly in mind as a 'good object', to use Melanie Klein's terminology. I supported Alan in preparing a goodbye ritual for his mother; he rehearsed his goodbye to her several times, perfecting this ritual for himself. We then went on to plan how this could become part of a 'real' service in his own church. I supported him in organising this as a memorial service at the church, with his own vicar, at which he read something which he had created in the therapy session; he also chose the music and hymns. This event culminated in the planting of a rose bush in her memory.

This piece of work took place over six months of weekly sessions and brought together two important elements identified in the initial assessment; that of taking control, which Alan achieved through planning the service himself, and also having a chance to say goodbye to his mother.

Once this work had been completed, we spent some time reminiscing on the things Alan had done in his life and how these activities had given him a sense of value. Alan had had several jobs when he was living in the long stay hospital. He had also secured a job in another hospital nearby, which he started two years before he was discharged and which continued for a further twenty-seven years; this had involved him travelling to the hospital from his home in the 'community'. He began to recognize the people who would remember him both from the past and from the present. We added these memories to his life book. I also did some educative work with him on funerals.

I eventually assessed that he seemed ready to end therapy. Alan no longer seemed so anxious and angry in the sessions, nor did he show a need to go over and over his memories of his mother; he appeared altogether calmer. We prepared to end the work over the next couple of months (ten months after we had begun). He seemed quite positive about this in our sessions together.

I then heard from several sources that outside the sessions, Alan was behaving oddly. He also began to arrive at sessions looking unkempt; his hair was dishevelled, and his clothes wrongly buttoned up. Over time he began to look unwell; he was dribbling, which he had never done before and this had led to his face becoming very sore. I telephoned his community nurse to check on his medication. I was told that it had been put up because Alan's anxiety levels had become extremely high (these had dropped right down during the course of the therapy); he had been stopping traffic and ranting to the drivers' about the dangers of the roads for pedestrians. I began to think that there was a connection to him ending his work with me and again feeling out of control and unsafe. The nurse told me that his medication was going to be increased again the next day, as there was such concern over him. I asked whether this could be postponed for a couple of days. I decided to reconsider the ending, thinking that I needed to assess whether finishing therapy was what was causing Alan's anxiety to rise. It was agreed that the nurse would reassess the situation once I had informed Alan of the reprieve.

In my session the next day I talked through some of my concerns with Alan and told him that we could have another three months in which to end. His whole posture and facial expression changed. He wanted me to take a photo of him; in this photo he is smiling and looks relaxed. We then went on to negotiate a new ending date that felt right for both of us. I contacted the nurse a few days later and the situation had completely changed; Alan was no longer behaving so anxiously. The next week I attended an emergency multidisciplinary meeting which was held to consider the best way of supporting Alan (which he also attended). I helped him to name some of the things that felt so out of control in his life. Some strategies for coping with these were drawn up collectively.

The way that Alan was supported during the last few months of the therapy illustrates how important it is for all the people involved in supporting someone to communicate clearly together, involving the person themselves wherever possible. In this way a consistent approach can be followed with everyone aware of the issues involved, and with the person with learning disabilities' best interests at the forefront. This is important, as it is so easy for different professionals or even family members to jealously fight their corner about what they feel is the right way forward without necessarily having the full picture. It is particularly easy for therapists or counsellors to work in isolation and to not be aware of the person's life outside the counselling room. If this had been the case for Alan, he could have gone downhill very rapidly, and all the good work that had taken place might have been undone. Instead it became a way for Alan to be enabled to take some control over his life, and also for him to recognize that all the people in the network around him were fully supportive of him doing this.

This experience led me to set up a project to restore and maintain the cemetery of one of the local long stay hospitals which had closed down several years previously. I contacted the local further education college's Special Needs department, and spoke to the tutor who ran a reminiscence course with the students. Many of the students were in their fifties or above and had spent a large part of their lives living in long stay hospitals. I knew that the group that she was running had recently visited a local cemetery in the community; this had brought up all sorts of issues for individuals in the group, but had also been a positive experience. The tutor was interested, and raised it with another staff member who runs a gardening class, and also informed me about a local organisation which hires out its gardening and landscaping services and is staffed by people with learning disabilities. The gardening organisation was enthusiastic about taking on the role of overseeing an annual maintenance programme and in issuing professional guidance to the college gardening group. The next step was to seek funding for this idea. I would hope that the cemetery might also become a place where the reminiscence group might come to visit. It is a very peaceful and beautiful place, and it may be helpful for some of the older survivors of the institutions to see that former patients have not been forgotten. It may give them some hope that they will not be either.

A life devalued

Marks (1999) describes how in western society the value of people's lives is often based on the level of useful contribution they are able to make to others. This leads to an assumption that when people are seen as being dependent or perceived as suffering their lives are not seen as worth living. She goes on to say that from this moral foundation, western medicine, which presents itself as treating everyone as equal, and as not taking a moral stance, 'perpetuates a range of practices which betray deep prejudices against those people who are defined as 'incurable 'and damaged.' (p. 50) It has been well documented that many people with learning disabilities are not receiving access to the same health care as the rest of the population, in particular to screening (Department of Health White Paper 2001, Mencap 1999), and many people with learning disabilities do not even have a GP. The result of this is that people are often diagnosed in the very late stages of a terminal illness where curative treatment is likely to be impossible. Because people with learning disabilities are now living longer (Jancar 1990) they are as likely as the rest of society to experience terminal illnesses such as cancer, cardio vascular or respiratory diseases. Yet research shows that they are less likely to receive the benefits of palliative care than other sections of society (Tuffrey-Wigne 2003).

A dilemma often emerges when someone with learning disabilities is diagnosed with a serious illness. People with learning disabilities, their families and the care staff supporting them often feel that they would be better off being cared for within the home setting rather than in hospital. This is because of the very real fear that society often takes the view that death would be a release, and that therefore the person might not receive prompt or efficient treatment, or even be treated with dignity or respect. (See Paul's story in Chapter 2). For people who have lived in long stay hospitals there can also be a fear of returning to a hospital environment. Palliative care at home can be a challenge to the palliative services that are beginning to wake up to the need. In my experience, palliative care services can often feel overwhelmed by learning disability services. They work in such different ways and yet it is so important for these two professions to find ways of supporting each other. It is also important that learning disability services invest trust in palliative care services and recognize when there is a need to hand someone over to the care of a hospice. Residential homes are not always set up to administer the kind of pain relief and care that someone who is close to the end of their life might need.

Todd (2002) helps us to think of the prejudices we often see against disability in the medical profession by considering the 'personal tragedy' and 'social' models of disability. He describes the former as carrying with it the view that death may be seen as a welcome release from an imperfect body, transforming loss into a gain. The social model on the other hand would recognise that death would bring with it 'a legitimate feeling of a loss of a valued part of one's life.' (p. 235)

The following description highlights how these two polarised views of disability can affect family members. The bereaved mother of Helen, a young woman who had been born with severe learning disabilities, described how she felt in the first year following Helen's death. She said that people around her imagined she would be relieved when her learning disabled daughter died, and expected her to get over the death very quickly. She felt angered by this, and said she had been affected very badly by Helen's death. In some ways she had been surprised by how long it had taken her to begin to feel she could get back to living her own life again.

She said she felt confused by the strength of her feelings after her daughter's death, because she recognised that sometimes when Helen was alive, she had felt that she hated her. Naturally, this was a difficult thing to admit. Since her death, Helen's mother had been able to realise that that it was actually the disability that she had hated, for all the strain it had put on her, on her daughter and on the entire family. She realised very clearly that she was mourning Helen the person; she recognised how much she loved her daughter, and how strong a connection she had with her.

The unspoken fears of Alan as described earlier in the chapter; *"Will anyone care when I die?"* has its roots in the voice of society that still places little value on the life of someone with a learning disability, and greets bereaved family members with thoughts such as *"Well, now you can get on with your life"* or, *"It's a blessing really; he didn't have much of a life, did he?"*

Chapter 10

Identifying training needs

The caring professions are not afforded much value by society, reflecting, it would seem, the status of those for whom they care. There is a tendency for this workforce to be made up of some of the most underprivileged and disempowered sections of the community. A high proportion of this group are women, often from ethnic minority groups. They mostly come into the work with very little training, are given very little supervision, are poorly paid and work long hard hours. And yet the job that is expected of them, if done well, is highly complex, ranging from basic cooking, cleaning and intimate care, through to implementing policies and procedures and supporting residents across a wide range of needs. The part of caring that is often given the least attention, perhaps because it is the most difficult, is that of supporting the residents' emotional needs.

There is irony in the fact that it is often people in a close supporting role: family, direct care staff and other professionals such as social workers, nurses and consultants, who can appear most likely to act in an unthinking way. That is to say, the very basic and obvious things that will affect the emotional well-being of an individual are not always fully considered. This is never so obvious as at the time of bereavement, when decisions have to be made regarding breaking the news of the death, or attending the funeral. Often the action taken is not as one would expect, under such circumstances. It seems to become extremely difficult for people to think through the issues clearly and rationally, or to take the emotional well-being of the individual into account, if that person has a learning disability.

As has been discussed throughout this book, both death and disability are surrounded by taboo and when these factors occur together, it seems people often do not know how to respond. They may prefer to believe that the person with a learning disability will not understand what has happened. People can sometimes not be told of the death of a parent for days, weeks, months or even longer. Sometimes they are refused final contact with a dying parent or are denied the chance to attend a funeral, all in the name of sparing their feelings or being for the 'best'. Would any of us wish this to be our experience?

In 1981 Strachan carried out a survey of bereaved residents in a large long stay hospital in Scotland, and recorded the general attitude of staff. He found that the staff felt that there was no point in discussing death with the residents because they "could not understand", or it might be " unnecessarily painful". They thought that they were doing the best thing; they were acting out of kindness. We could see it as ignorance or we could look at it from a purely political stance and call it discrimination. But if we were to examine it more deeply and to really try to understand why this sort of thing happens, not only back in the '70s and '80s but happening still today, then maybe we could start to bring about change. Why are we continuing to be so stupid?

Sinason (1992) reminds us of the original meaning of the word 'stupid'. She states that when we re-examine the meaning, it is of no surprise that many people with learning disabilities choose to use the word to describe themselves. The original meaning is 'numbed with grief'. Sinason (1992) states that the original meaning of the word 'shines through' because 'a lot of the pain and secondary effects of handicap are to do with the grief of internal and external trauma' (p. 43).

But even more interestingly, when she discusses her experience of working with staff from learning disability settings, Sinason highlights an important phenomenon. She describes how people behave when attending her workshops or training days. They begin by apologizing for their lack of knowledge and lack of training (regardless of their level of seniority or professional background); they then show that in actual fact, they know a great deal about the difficulties of their clients. Gradually they start revealing extracts from some of the many horror stories they carry on behalf of their clients. Finally, they become aware that they said they knew nothing because they knew a lot, and could not bear what they knew when they felt unable to change very much for the people for whom they were caring.

Thus when we come back to trying to understand why people act so 'stupidly' around bereaved people with learning disabilities, could it be that the added pain of bereavement, on top of what they have already seen and experienced, is too painful to bear? That they become 'stupefied'? An important point raised by the staff attending Sinason's training is the overwhelming feeling of helplessness that people experience on a number of levels, when they are with someone with a learning disability. It may be a helplessness to know how to communicate, or to be able to change the circumstances, or it may just be the fact that being with someone with a disability brings up all sorts of very powerful feelings of being de-skilled or 'disabled' oneself.

Simpson (2002) describes how for many people with learning disabilities, development of learning becomes arrested. He elaborates by describing how, whilst working with an adolescent boy in psychotherapy, he became aware of the boy's unconscious fear of the therapist's thinking and curiosity. Simpson's theory is that if curiosity is aroused in either the child or the care-giver, this may bring about feelings of guilt and shame in each of them regarding the cause and/or consequences of the disability. The disabled child therefore remains in a perpetual state of infancy, unable to take the risk of being curious, in order to protect both itself and the parent (carer) from this awareness and the painful feelings. If we think about this psychodynamically, transference of this kind to all care-givers may be very strong, especially to residential support staff. This may be another way to understand what was going on in Sinason's training sessions, described above.

Since de-institutionalisation, about one third of the UK adult population of people with learning disabilities live in staffed residential houses. Research has shown that there is a higher turnover of staff in residential homes in the community than there was in the large institutions (Allen et al 1990). This leads to inconsistent care and to fragmented relationships. Investing in practical, meaningful training for this workforce would be a healthy option for all concerned - the workers, the people they serve and also for the financial viability of services. The provision of regular 'clinical' supervision is also important. The kind of supervision required is not solely task-focused, but one which also provides a space to air feelings, to consider and reflect on the meaning of interactions with service users and the nature of key-working relationships. Below are some of the elements that could go towards making up a sound, robust training programme for all direct care staff. They are designed to strengthen the ability of a team to support the emotional well being of those in their care.

1 A basic understanding of psychodynamic theory and its relevance to disability.

I would propose that all direct care staff and other hands-on professionals are given a basic training on the value of trying to understand interactions with the people that they are supporting from a psychodynamic perspective. This would aid them in trying to make sense of what can sometimes be a very intense and confusing role, and provide them with some emotional distance. A psychodynamic perspective is also an important tool in understanding interactions with people who are non-verbal, and people with profound learning disabilities. A foundation in this way of thinking would also provide a good underpinning to clinical supervision.

If entire staff teams were equipped with a basic understanding of psychodynamic thinking, everyone could work from the same perspective. Training would include an explanation of transference and counter-transference and its relevance to understanding some of the uncomfortable feelings that can occur in support work. Guidance on the importance of clinical supervision, and how best to use it, would also be useful.

2 Understanding the care worker relationship

Keyworking in residential or day care can be a confusing and demanding job. It can often be difficult to define the boundaries and to understand the dynamics at play within the relationship between worker and client. This is especially so in residential settings, where staff may sleep and eat in the same setting as residents.

Bowlby (1988) states that the ability to offer effective care depends on the degree to which individuals have received it themselves. We cannot always be sure of the motivation for people coming into caring professions, or of their own personal experience of receiving care when young. But what can be addressed is an awareness of attachment theory and how early attachments influence adult relationships. This may enable staff to work with a little more understanding of how difficult it often is for people with learning disabilities to make and maintain relationships. This should also include thinking about preparations regarding the ending of key-working relationships (Mattison and Pistrang 2000).

3 Bereavement awareness

All staff in residential and day services should be provided with Loss and Bereavement training. In general terms, this should provide a basic understanding of the grief process and enable staff to work proactively with clients in preparation for an expected death. It would cover information on loss and bereavement and look at how this may specifically affect people with learning disabilities. It is usually best to offer a mixture of theory and interactive techniques encouraging participants to draw on their own experience of loss, in order to recognize the variety of coping mechanisms that come into effect at the time of a trauma. Ideally, then, the training should be designed to help staff to consider the impact of their own experience of loss; recognizing their personal vulnerabilities and how this may impact on them professionally, and enabling them to acknowledge when they are in need of personal support. Another aim would be to enable staff to recognise stress from past bereavements in their clients and to work compassionately, but also to know when to refer clients on for more specialised help. As I have already stressed, direct care staff can make a real difference to the outcome of an individual's bereavement, depending on the quality of the support given and on the awareness and understanding informing decisions and actions taken.

This training should include the check list of key features below:

- **A basic understanding of grief**. This is best taught using a simple model such as stages and/or tasks (Worden), emphasizing that there is no set path through these. Stroebe's model may also be used in order to think about restoration orientation work. (See Chapter 1)
- **Consideration about the importance of funerals** is invaluable in enabling staff to support residents in future decisions
- Participants should be given an opportunity to consider their own ways of coping with loss in order to recognize the **varied coping styles of each individual.** Participants also need to recognize their own loss history, and how this may hinder or help their ability to support others
- **The specific complications surrounding parental bereavement for someone with a learning disability** should also be given some focus, in the context of **attachment**
- Information on **concurrent losses and bereavement behaviours** should be provided

- The training should also enable teams to have a clearer idea as to when or if there is a **need to refer individuals for a psychological intervention** on future occasions
- The training could also precipitate the drawing up of or the dissemination of **a policy on bereavement specific to the service**
- The development of **creative startegies** encouraging people to remember others from the service who have died or left. McEnhill (1999) suggests, for example, creating a wall of photographs.

If all residential and day services have protocols to follow on bereavement, workers' sensitivity will be heightened to this issue. Ideally this would mean that everyone working closely with service users would know their current situation, in addition to their loss history.

Policies should include:

1 Recording a bereavement and loss history of everyone using the service. This should be kept with the person's file and should be updated regularly
2 Procedures around the breaking of bad news
3 Designating a named member of staff whom the service user trusts to be the person they can talk to when they are feeling sad
4 Providing bereavement training for staff
5 Providing support in the form of regular supervision and access to counselling services for staff

An example of good practice regarding this is to be found in Nottingham Health Care NHS Trust (UK). This unit carried out an evaluation to find out current practice in residential services when a person with a learning disability had been bereaved. This identified good practice as well as areas of concern, and noted what services were being offered by other professionals. The findings were then looked at alongside theory and current research in the field. The ideas generated from this resulted in a set of draft guidelines which were then piloted. An audit was carried out to find out which practices had been effective and which had not, resulting in a comprehensive set of guidelines on good practice published in 2000. These are now used in a consistent way throughout Nottingham. They are a useful resource for all. (See Resource List)

4 Training in awareness of the mental health of people with learning disabilities

As has been highlighted already in this book (Chapter 4), bereaved people with learning disabilities are vulnerable to mental distress. Staff often have no formal training and very little experience to draw on for this. Yet alongside the family, it is recognized that since staff have the closest and most regular contact with the people with learning disabilities they support, they are in the best position to detect the smallest changes in behaviour that might be indicative of mental distress.

A report made to the Department of Health in 1995 by the Hester Adrian Research Centre recommended that provision needed to be made for the training of direct care staff, in order that they could recognise when there was a need to refer individuals for appropriate psychiatric assessment. New and sensitive techniques for the assessment and screening of mental health in adults with intellectual disabilities have been produced and developed. There are tools for detecting early dementia, such as the PAS-ADD (Moss et al 1993) and the Mini PAS-ADD. The latter can be used by health and social service staff to help them identify mental health problems in the people they care for. Training materials have also been designed (Menolascino et al 1992. Dosen 1994) for direct care staff in order to raise awareness and under-standing of mental illness in people with intellectual disabilities.

5 The importance of building and strengthening social networks

An important part of coping for many people when they are bereaved is to turn to friends and family, and yet for someone who is learning disabled, this can often be very difficult or impossible. Most people with learning disabilities have small and fragile social networks (Atkinson 1989, Flynn, 1989, Firth and Rapley 1990, Chappell 1994) as has been described in earlier chapters. If the person is lucky enough to still have a family who is in contact with them, or if they have recently left the family home, their social life may be almost entirely built around family and may also include the people who they see every day at the day-centre or college. When a parent dies this whole network can easily disintegrate, especially if the person then moves away from where they were living and has to change day services. This can leave the person even more isolated.

The first and most important step is to recognize the existing networks that the person has and for these to be valued. Wherever possible steps to maintain these relationships should be put in place. When a parent dies, it may be important to establish whether there were any neighbours with whom there has been a long-standing or special relationship, which church or synagogue congregation they are a part of, and so on. In other words, which communities did the parent provide a bridge into for their family member with a learning disability, when they were alive? It is important to ask this sort of question in order that these ties are not lost.

Services may have to be creative about how these bonds can be kept alive. Research indicates that many people only see their friends at colleges or in the day service: there is very little contact outside these structures.

> For reasons that are not immediately obvious, quite able people
> with apparently good communication skills would not consider
> asking someone they know back to their home, or arrange to see
> them outside the environment in which they meet ordinarily.
>
> Pettingell & Hart 2001, p. 342

If there are any remaining family members, they may not live nearby and may not visit often. The person with learning disabilities is likely to have few friends and they may find it difficult to maintain contact with those that they have (within day-centres for example). If an individual seeks out friendships with non-learning disabled people, however, this in itself may be fraught with difficulties. People may seek to become friends with members of staff (Mattison and Pistrang 2000) or put themselves in vulnerable positions, singling out people that they hardly know and being over-familiar, or call virtual strangers their friends. The external and practical difficulties are a different matter and something to which staff need to give consideration. If people were given straightforward practical support, this picture might change. People in residential services often have restricted access to their own money, which can make it difficult to go to the pub with friends, for example.

Transport is another obvious barrier to people's social independence; not everyone has had the support to learn to use public transport, and for some people this would not be an option. Even people who do use it can often feel justifiably vulnerable using it at night. There is evidence to show that people with learning disabilities are often the target of opportunistic crimes such as mugging, or just plain bullying and harassment. Using taxis is another very real possibility although these come with their own frustrations, such as not turning up when they are booked or arriving late. The whole issue of transport is in itself a powerful metaphor for dependency. In my experience, transport is often the issue that can provoke the most upset for people.

Some people would need the support of staff in accompanying them to social engagements, but staff rotas, willingness or awareness do not always facilitate this. It may also be difficult for people to invite friends home, due to lack of privacy or to staff not welcoming this. People with learning disabilities are often very passive in social connections, relying instead on others to make things happen; this may be due to a lack of skills and practice. There are a number of skills needed to make social arrangements. The person needs to be able to initiate contact at the outset, whether by telephone or in a letter. Both are difficult in their own way, and people may need support to do either of these things. One obvious difficulty is knowing the contact details of the other person in the first place, and the person may need support to find out this information. They then need to be able to negotiate a convenient date and time for both parties to meet, and finally they need to be able to remember this date once it is arranged, and get to the meeting place on time.

All in all, organizing an independent social life is complicated, and people may need considerable support to do this. It is clear that more focus and emphasis should be put into developing these skills by staff. It would be useful for staff to attend training which encouraged them to look at ways of enabling people with learning disabilities to learn the skills required to maintain friendships. For example, learning to support people with learning disabilities to develop telephone skills to make the arrangements to meet up, and for staff to understand and be able to provide the necessary support to follow this through. Staff can also take basic practical steps such as enabling the people they are supporting to keep an accessible and up-to-date record of friends' and relatives' telephone numbers.

If service settings and frameworks placed more emphasis on this sort of action by staff rather than the need to have a choice of two puddings every night or have colour co-ordinated curtains and wallpaper, I firmly believe there would be less loneliness in the lives of people with learning disabilities.

Beyond residential services
The next section is written with other professionals in mind. The first part is aimed at education, health and social services, particularly those services which support families at the time of transition from schools into adult services, but also at any other time when it may be possible to support a proactive move from the family home. It is so much healthier all round if this move can be a considered choice, rather than effected during a crisis brought about through bereavement. The second part is aimed at generic services, for example counselling and bereavement services or mainstream health settings, so that professionals within these agencies might think about extending their services to people with learning disabilities.

Families and transitions
A report by the Foundation for People with Learning Disabilities (2003) states:

> One of the biggest worries for family carers is what will happen when they are no longer able to care for their relative with a learning disability   (p. 2)

It is estimated that one third of people with learning disabilities living in the family home are living with a carer over the age of seventy or more (2001 UK Government White Paper *Valuing People*). For older families, the thought of their adult child leaving home may have very different implications than for younger families, and may be more difficult to think about. Families may need support and encouragement to think about a time when their learning disabled adult children could stop living with the family, and move into their own home.

Older parents may have kept their children at home with them against all the odds, where perhaps in the past, professionals were strongly advising them to leave their offspring in the long-stay institution and forget all about them. There may well therefore be a lot of pain around the idea of letting their child leave the safety of the family home. The parents may never want to consider the prospect of their family member with a learning disability ever living anywhere other than with them, secretly hoping that they will outlive their child. It is important to consider that older family carers may have experienced decades of neglectful treatment or worse by services, and this will quite rightly have made them protective of their adult child and suspicious of professionals. In these situations, a sincere sensitivity to the family's history is vital. There is also a different consideration to take into account. Older parents may be receiving a lot of support and practical care from their adult child, which in turn gives the person with the learning disability a very valuable role. In these situations, great care should be taken not to break apart this fragile interdependence.

However, it is also important to recognise the reality that a large percentage of people with learning disabilities are outliving their parents. If families are not supported to think about this very real probability before the time comes, the person with a learning disability could be faced with a crisis move. I have described elsewhere in this book the many complications which can occur when people have to move suddenly, as a parent becomes ill or dies. It is therefore preferable, wherever possible, for trusting relationships between professionals and families to be built up gradually over a period of time. It is only within a trusting relationship that it could become possible for the whole family to consider the future together, to bear to think of a time when they will no longer be able to continue living in the same way and to make some informed choices about what might happen (see Chapter 5).

Planned transitions can be successful for all concerned, but take a lot of preparation and need to move at the right pace of all the individuals involved. It will require a proactive approach on behalf of professionals, which may not be easy, especially when parents have been coping for decades on their own with very little support from services. Some families become 'hidden', and only become known when there is a crisis, such as the death of a parent or when a parent becomes too frail to manage any more (2003 Report from FPWLD). The UK Government White Paper *Valuing People* (2001) has identified older carers as a priority for learning disability services to support and include in decision-making. The report on older family carers by the Foundation for People with Learning Disabilities suggests that there is an urgent need:

... for learning disability services to make stronger links with older people's social and primary health care services, to provide a joined-up approach to supporting older family carers.

(2003 p. 5)

For families with younger learning disabled adults, it is useful for professionals to begin to think about and discuss options with families at around the age that most young people might be thinking of leaving home, perhaps any time from eighteen years through to the mid-twenties. This might entail taking families to visit a variety of residential services in the area, meeting with other families who have experienced a successful transition, even setting up family groups in order to discuss all the concerns and feelings around transition.

Providing disability training for generic therapists and counsellors
Another area of importance to address through training is that of enabling generic professionals to consider making their services available to people with learning disabilities (see also Chapters 2 and 6)

The UK Government White Paper *Valuing People* (2001) stresses that people with learning disabilities should be able to access mainstream services. We are still a long way from this becoming a reality. With regard to therapeutic and counselling services, it is only in the last decade or so that people with learning disabilities could expect to be offered any sort of therapy other than a behavioural approach. Traditionally it was thought that people with a low IQ would not be able to benefit from psychotherapy or counselling. The recent study by the Royal College of Psychiatry Working Group - United Kingdom and Ireland (2002) shows that this view has been challenged by pioneering work from professionals at St George's Hospital Medical School and the Tavistock Clinic (see Chapter 6). It also shows that there are a number of innovative services being developed. The report states that psychotherapy is delivered by many disciplines and in many modes. However, this development is still mainly confined to specialist learning disability services. The next step is to find ways of encouraging generic therapists and counsellors to open up their services to people with learning disabilities.

There are a few services across the country where this is beginning to happen. *Extend* in St.Albans, and *The Shoulder Project* in Stoke, have been fine examples of mainstream counselling services adapting their service to include people with learning disabilities, although recently both seem to have been adversely affected by financial difficulties.

There are several factors which can prevent people with learning disabilities accessing services. Finance is an obvious one, but others are more subtle and include preconceived ideas about learning disability, inaccessible information and/or inaccessible location, inflexibility of practice, and difficulties regarding communication. Some of these issues could be addressed through training.

I was recently approached by a colleague and friend who has a learning disability. She expressed an interest in co-writing and co-facilitating a Loss and Bereavement course together. She has her own personal experience of bereavement and of receiving bereavement counselling, and I have experience of providing a bereavement therapy service to people with learning disabilities and also of delivering staff training. The aim would be to combine our skills and knowledge in order to offer training to mainstream therapists and counsellors in the hope that they will then consider extending their services to people with a learning disability.

In considering what we would include in this type of training, we have needed to think about some of the issues mentioned above and how these might be addressed. One of the particularly strong points about this training would be the inclusion of my co-facilitator, a woman who herself has learning disabilities. I can think of no better way to confront and dispel myths and prejudice around learning disability than to include people themselves in delivering the training, especially to people who may have had very little experience in getting to know anyone with a learning disability.

Below is a list of some of the elements that would need to be included in a training day for generic counsellors:

- **Terminology** - ever-shifting within the field of learning disability. Terms can be confusing, and it would therefore be useful to explore terminology in a historical context. This could help prevent counsellors becoming so tied up in political correctness that they lose focus on their client as a person.
- A brief overview of the **history of learning disability**
- **Attachment and disability**

- The **particular vulnerabilities of people with learning disability** at a time of **bereavement**
- **Transference and countertransference**
- **Styles of communication**
- The use of **creative methods**

Raising awareness in mainstream health services
There is a need to raise the awareness of the needs of people with learning disabilities in mainstream health settings such as GP surgeries, hospitals, hospices and so on, in order that the unconscious death wish towards people with learning disabilities is not acted out (see Chapter 2). By providing training and information to professionals who have little previous knowledge of learning disability, perspectives can be shifted. There is some pioneering work being done at St George's Teaching Hospital in London (UK), where training on how to work sensitively with patients who have a learning disability is a standard part of the course for all doctors in training. Much of this is delivered directly by people with learning disabilities themselves. There is also a need for recognition of the importance of partnership working in these settings, between the health services and the learning disability services, and also the importance of the role of families. Family members and learning disability staff often have extensive knowledge of the intimate needs of individuals and of the particular communication style that the person may use. It is therefore important that health professionals build working relationships with the support networks that surround individuals in their care, in order to make health interventions as stress free as possible for a patient with learning disabilities who may already be experiencing stress as result of being unwell.

This chapter has provided pointers towards areas of training and development which, once addressed, would enable people with learning disabilities to be given support in a way which would recognize and value their emotional lives. It describes the importance of pro-active planning and preparation in order for the best possible outcomes to be achieved.

For too long, services for people with learning disabilities have ignored the importance of acknowledging and responding to the feelings of the people with learning disabilities and the importance of valuing their relationships. I hope that this book will be a contribution towards bringing about a change in these attitudes. I offer the following example of a piece of work I carried out with a young bereaved man, to remind us of the difference that conscious support can bring about.

John is a man in his late twenties, who lived in his family home all his life. He was referred to the Loss and Bereavement Service where I work after the sudden and traumatic death of his mother, which had resulted in John being moved immediately to a large group home quite a distance away from his home. His father had died five years earlier.

John's mother had done everything for him throughout his life. She anticipated what he wanted before he needed to ask. Food appeared on the table before he knew he was hungry, and his clothes were chosen and laid out for him. John suffers from epilepsy, and his mother would spot a minor 'absence' almost before he was aware of it himself; she would offer him the necessary support without him having to communicate that anything was wrong.

Since his father's death, John had lived on his own with his mother. They led a routine and ordered life, doing the shopping together on the same day each week. John mixed with his mother's friends; he also saw his siblings regularly, as they lived nearby. He had chosen not to pursue specialised daytime services (such as attending a day-centre), preferring instead to be at home, out alone or with his mother. Whilst living at home, he would often walk independently into town and spend time there just walking about; he knew his way around confidently, and was a known member of the community.

Suddenly, after his mother's death, John found himself living in a large institutionalised setting. This meant that he had to share everything with the many other residents, and had to interact with a large and ever-changing staff group. John not only had to deal with grieving for the loss of his mother, but he also had to adapt to an enormous number of changes to his everyday life. He had to get used to a new location and environment, a new routine (he was expected to go to a day-centre every day), new people, sharing with others rather than being the one who was doted on, and perhaps hardest of all, new expectations of him from unfamiliar others. Staff in his new home described John as surly, lazy, uncooperative and selfish. It is sobering to imagine how any of us might react in such circumstances.

It is a generally accepted fact that it is unwise for people at a time of bereavement to make any major lifestyle changes (Worden 1983), and yet as we have seen throughout this book, people with learning disabilities are so often given no choice. Perhaps the behaviours that staff described at the point of referral were actually symptoms of depression. This would be an understandable response to all the sudden changes John had undergone.

Another complicating factor for John was that his mother had died very unexpectedly when they had been at home together, and he had been alone with her body for three days until the situation was discovered by one of his sisters. When the referral was made, John said very little about what had happened during the 'lost' time. When his sister discovered her mother's death, she was naturally very upset. Along with other people, she could not understand why John had not sought help earlier on, since on many levels, he is a very able young man.

For many of the early therapy sessions, John sat silently. His mood seemed sullen. He seemed full of guilt for his mother's death, and he felt that people were angry with him (an accurate perception). He found the whole experience impossible to talk about. There was a deadness about him, a lack of vitality; he was very thin, looked unkempt, his hair was lank and greasy and he had no pride in what he wore. There was an added difficulty in these early sessions; this was the lack of commitment from the staff supporting him. I felt that they really did not like John, and that perhaps unconsciously, they sabotaged his sessions by bringing him late, or sometimes not bringing him at all. But I felt strong feelings of protectiveness towards John (my countertransference) and saw him as a lost litle boy, at sea in his new surroundings. He seemed numb with grief. This made me determined to work hard on building a therapeutic relationship with him.

It was clear that part of the task of supporting John in his grief was to enable the mainly young and untrained staff from the residential setting to understand and appreciate some of the factors involved in John's situation, particularly the losses connected to his lifestyle at home. In order that they might perceive John's behaviour differently, and less judgmentally, two training days were set up as part of the bereavement package, but due to the high turnover of workers in this setting, additional consultation was also provided as ongoing support for staff. Once this was in place, the staff become more able to empathise with John, and instead of provoking conflict, enabled him to develop the skills of sharing with others and the ability to recognize and state his own needs.

John's therapy sessions gained momentum once the staff training was completed. The staff became far more committed to John, and he was supported to come to his sessions regularly. Much of the work I did with John in our early sessions together was carried out in a distanced way. I did not talk with him directly about his mother's death, but instead we worked on stories and paintings. These did not seem to be connected to his mother, but they gave me a chance to understand his feelings, and this non-threatening activity gave us both something on which the therapeutic relationship could be built. John was quite clever with numbers, and he was always keen to demonstrate these skills to me; sometimes sessions were devoted to John's numerical skills. As he said very little during most of the early sessions, I had to rely on the countertransference feelings that I was experiencing in relation to John to understand anything about his thoughts and feelings.

John stayed in therapy with me for longer than the average client, part-ly due to the traumatic experience of his bereavement and its effect on him. We worked together for over two years. It was not until the second year that he could tolerate me asking about the death of his mother. During the two years he had began to talk far more in our sessions, his appearance changed, he began to take more pride in how he looked and had far more of a sense of aliveness about him.

Over the course of our one-to-one work together, and with good support from the staff, John was able to change. He began to learn to recognise his feelings, state his needs, and to share; this has led to him being able to lead a more independent life.

I hope that the stories such as John's above, which have been so gener-ously and bravely shared, will have an impact on those who read them. I hope also this will in turn empower some people to feel brave enough to act, in whatever capacity they are able, in order to bring about at least one small positive change in the lives of the people with learning disabilities that they support.

References

Accardo, P. & Whitman, B. (1990) Children of mentally retarded parents *American Journal of Diseases of Children*, 144: 69-70

Ainsworth, M. D. S., Bell, S. M., & Stayton, D. J, (1974) Infant-mother attachment and social development: socialization as a product of reciprocal responsiveness to signals in *The Integration of a Child into a Social World* Richards, M. (Ed.) Cambridge: Cambridge University Press

Allen, P., Pahl, J. & Quine, L. (1990) *Care Staff in Transition: The Impact on Staff of Changing Services for People with Mental Handicaps.* London: HMSO

Allington-Smith, P., Ball, R. & Haytor, R. (2002) Management of sexually abused children with learning disabilities *Advances in Psychiatric Treatment*, 8: 66-72

Ashman, A. F., Suttie, J. N. & Bramley, J. (1995) Employment, retirement and elderley persons with an intellectual disability *Journal of Intellectual Disability Research*, 39: 107-115

Atkinson, D. (1989) *Someone to Turn to: The Social Worker's Role and the Role of Front-line Staff in Relation to People with Mental Handicaps* Kidderminster: British Institute of Mental Handicap Publications

Averill, J. R. (1968) Grief: its nature and significance *Psychological Bulletin*, 70 (6): 721-48

Bank-Mikkelson, N. (1980) Denmark, in R. Flynn & K. Nitsch (Eds) *Normalisation, Social Integration and Community Services* Austin, Texas: Pro-Ed

Barnes, C. (1994) *Disabled People in Britain and Discrimination: A Case for Anti-Discrimination Legislation* London: Hurst and Company, in Association with BCODP

Beail, N. (1998) Psychoanalytic psychotherapy with men with intellectual disabilities: a preliminary outcome study *British Journal of Medical Psychology*, 71: 1-11

Bicknell, J. (1983) The psychopathology of handicap. *British Journal of Medical Psychology*, (56)167-178

Bihm E, M and Elliot L, S. (1982) Conceptions of death in mentally retarded persons. *Journal of Psychology*, 111: 205-210

Bion, W. Attacks on linking, *International Journal of Psychoanalysis* 40: 308-15 republished in *The Psychoanalytical Study of Thinking* Bion (1967) pp. 93-109

Blackman, N. (1999) The roc Loss and Bereavement Therapeutic Service in *Living with Loss: Helping People with Learning Disabilities Cope with Bereavement and Loss* Blackman, N. (Ed.) Brighton UK: Pavilion Publishing

Blackman, N. (2000) Dramatherapy with people with learning disabilities in a Loss and Bereavement Therapy Service, Chapter 9, pp. 111-120 in *Assessment and Evaluation in the Arts Therapies: Art Therapy, Music Therapy and Dramatherapy* Wigram T. (Ed.) Radlett UK: Harper House Publications

Blackman, N. (2002) Grief and intellectual disability: a systemic approach. *Journal of Gerontological Social Work* (38) No.s 1&2: 253-263

Bonell-Pascuel, E., Huline-Dickens, S., Hollins, S., Esterhuyzen, A., Sedwick, P., Abdelnoor, A. & Hubert, J. (1999) Bereavement and grief in adults with learning disabilities: a follow-up study *British Journal of Psychiatry*, 175: 348-350

Booth, T. & Booth, W. (1994) *Parenting Under Pressure: Mothers and Fathers with Learning Disabilities* Buckingham, UK: Open University Press

Bowlby, J. (1960) Grief and mourning in infancy and early childhood. *Psychoanalytic Study of the Child*, 15: 9-52

Bowlby, J. (1963) Pathological mourning and childhood mourning *Journal of the American Psychoanalytic Association*, 11: 500-541

Bowlby, J. (1973) *Attachment and Loss: Volume 2, Separation, Anxiety and Anger* St Ives UK: Penguin Books

Bowlby, J. (1979) *The Making and Breaking of Affectional Bonds* London: Tavistock

Bowlby, J. (1980) *Attachment and Loss: Volume 3, Loss, Sadness and Depression* New York: Basic Books

Bowlby, J. (1988) *A Secure Base: Clinical Applications of Attachment Theory* London: Routledge

Bowlby, J. & Parkes, C. M. (1970) Separation and loss within the family, in *The Child in his Family* E. J. Anthony, E.J. & Koupernick, C. (Eds.) New York: Wiley

Bowman, T. (1994) Using poetry, fiction, and essays to help people face shattered dreams *Journal of Poetry Therapy*, 8 (2): 81-89

Brownell, P. and Congress, E. (1998) Application of the Culturagram to assess and empower culturally and ethnically diverse battered women, in *Battered Women and their Families* (2nd Edn.) Roberts, A. (Ed.) New York: Springer

Buchsbaum, B. C. (1996) Remembering a parent who has died: a developmental perspective, in *Continuing Bonds* Klass, D., Silverman, P. S. & Nickman, S. L (Eds.) Philadelphia, USA: Taylor and Francis

Butler, R. (1963) The life review: an interpretation of reminiscence in the aged, *Psychiatry: Journal for the Study of Interpersonal Processes* 26 (1): 65-76

Carlsson, B., Hollins, S., Nilsson, A., & Sinason, V., (2002) Preliminary findings; an Anglo-Swedish psychoanalytic psychotherapy outcome study using PORT and DMT Tizard Learning Disability Review 7(4): Oct

Cathcart, F. (1995) Death and people with learning disabilities: interventions to support clients and carers *British Journal of Clinical Psychology* 34: 165-175

Chappell, A. L. (1994) A question of friendship: community care and the relationships of people with learning difficulties *Disability and Society* 9: 419

Chapple, E.D. (1970) *Culture and Biological Man: Explorations in Behavioral Anthropology* New York: Holt, Rinehart and Winston

Chisholm, D. (1998) Costs and outcomes of the psychotherapeutic approaches to the treatment of mental disorders. *Mental Health Research Review* 5: 53-55

Clark, A. (2000) Insurance risks in The story of life. *The mapping of the human genome*, Special Supplement, The Guardian Newspaper, UK, June 26th, p.11

Conboy-Hill (1992) Grief, loss and people with learning disabilities, in *Psychotherapy and Mental Handicap* Waitman, A. & Conboy-Hill, S. (Eds.) London: Sage

Cooley, W. C., Graham, E. S., Moeschler, J. B. & Graham, J. M. (1990) Reactions of mothers and medical professionals to a film about Down Syndrome *American Journal of Disabled Children*, 144: 1112-1116

Craft, A. (1980) *Educating Mentally Handicapped People* London: Camera Talks Ltd

Craft, A. & Craft, M. (1979) *Handicapped Married Couples.* Oxford UK: Routledge and Kegan Paul Ltd

Craft, M. & Craft, A. (1983) *Sex Education and Counselling for Mentally Handicapped People.* Tunbridge Wells, UK: Costello

Craine, L. S., Henson, C. E., Colliver, J. A., & MacLean, D. G. (1988) Prevalence of a history of sexual abuse among female psychiatric patients in a state hospital system *Hospital and Community Psychiatry* 39: 300-304

Deutsch, H. (1937) The absence of grief *Psychoanalytic Quarterly*, 6: 12-22

Deutsch, H. (1985) Grief counselling with the mentally retarded clients *Psychiatric Aspects of Mental Retardation Reviews*, 4 (5): p17-20

Doka, K. (1989) *Disenfranchised Grief: Recognising Hidden Sorrow* USA: Lexington Books

Douglas, M. (1975) *Implicit Meaning* London: Routledge and Kegan Paul

Emde, R. (1983) The pre-representational self and its affective core. *The Psychoanalytic Study of the Child* 38: 165-192 New Haven: Yale University Press

Emerson, P. (1977) Covert grief reaction in mentally retarded clients *Mental Retardation*, 15: 46-47

Epstein, L. & Feiner, A. H. (1979) Countertransference: the therapist's contribution to treatment: an overview *Contemporary Psychoanalysis*, 15: 489-513

Finkelstein, V. (1980) *Attitudes and Disabled People: Issues for Discussion* N Y: World Rehabilitation Fund

Firth, H. & Rapley, M. (1990) *From Acquaintance to Friendship: Issues for people with learning disabilities* Kidderminster: British Institute of Mental Handicap Publications

Fletcher, A. (2001) *Considered Choices: The new genetics, prenatal testing and people with learning disabilities* Ward, L. (Ed.) Kidderminster, UK: BILD Publications

Flynn, M.C. (1989) *Independent Living for Adults with Mental Handicap: A place of my own* London: Cassell

Frankish, P. (1992) A psychodynamic approach to emotional difficulties within a social framework *Journal of Intellectual Disability Research* 36: 295-305

Freud, S. (1910) The future prospects of psychoanalytic psychotherapy in J. Strachey, (Ed. & Trans.) *The Standard Edition of the Complete Psychological Works of Sigmund Freud*(1957) (11) London: Hogarth Press

Freud, S. (1912) Recommendations for physicians practicing psychoanalysis in J. Strachey, (Ed. & Trans.) *The Standard Edition of the Complete Psychological Works of Sigmund Freud*(1957) (12) London: Hogarth

Freud, S. (1913) Totem and Taboo, *Collected Papers* London: Hogarth Press
Freud, S. (1915) Our attitude towards death, in J. Strachey, (Ed. & Trans.) *The Standard Edition of the Complete Psychological Works of Sigmund Freud* (14)   London: Hogarth Press
Freud, S. (1929) Inhibitions, Symptoms and Anxiety *Collected Papers* London: Hogarth Press London
Freud, S. (1961) Mourning and Melancholia in J. Strachey, (Ed. & Trans.) *The Standard Edition of the Complete Psychological Works of Sigmund Freud* (14) London: Hogarth Press. (original work 1917)
Furman, E. (1974) *A Child's Parent Dies: Studies in Childhood Bereavement* New Haven, CT: Yale University Press
Furman, R.A. (1973) A child's capacity for mourning, in *The Child and his Family* Anthony, E. & Koupernik, C. (Eds.) New York: Wiley
Gallagher, H. G. (1990) *By Trust Betrayed: Patients and Physicians in the Third Reich* London: Henry Hold.
Gersie, A. (1983) Story-telling and its links with the unconscious. A story about stories in *Dramatherapy* 7(1): 7-12
Gersie, A. (1984) "Have your dream of life come true" Myth-making in therapeutic practice in *Dramatherapy* 7(2): 3-10
Gersie, A. (1989) Stories and Therapy in Medlicott, M., *By word of mouth: the revival of storytelling*. London: Channel 4 Television
Gersie, A. (1991) *Storymaking in Bereavement* London: Jessica Kingsley Publishers
Gersie, A. (1997) *Reflections on Therapeutic Storymaking: The Use of Stories in Groups*. London: Jessica Kingsley Publishers
Gersie, A. (2003) Therapeutic Storymaking, in *The Prompt – The magazine of the British Association of Dramatherapists*. Winter 02/03
Gersie, A., King, N. (1990) *Storymaking in Education and Therapy*. Stockholm: Stockholm University Press and London: Jessica Kingsley Publishers
Gomez, L. (1997) *An Introduction to Object Relations* London: Free Association Books
Gordon, S. (1972) Sex education symposium *Journal of Special Education* 5: 351-381
Gravestock, S. & McGauley, G. (1994) Connecting confusions with painful realities: group analytic psychotherapy for adults with learning disabilities. *Psychoanalytic Psychotherapy* 8 (2): 153-167
Hannam, C. (1999) 'David' in Blackman, N. (Ed.) *Living with Loss: Helping People with Learning Disabilities Cope with Bereavement and Loss* Brighton :Pavilion Publishing
Harper, D.C. & Wadsworth, J. S. (1993) Grief in adults with mental retardation: preliminary findings *Research in Developmental Disabilities*, 14: 313-330
Haviland, W.H. (1978) *Cultural Anthropology* New York: John Wiley and Sons
Heimann, P. (1950) On countertransference *International Journal of Psychoanalysis* 31: 81-84
Helm, D. T., Miranda, S. & Angoff Chedd, N. (1998) *Mental Retardation* 36 (1): 55-61
Hodges, S. (2003) *Counselling Adults with Learning Disabilities* Hampshire, UK: Palgrave MacMillan
Hollins, S. (1998) *Bereavement and People with Learning Disabilities* A paper presented at a Conference on Palliative care and People with Learning disabilities organised by Marie Curie Cancer Care and Mencap in London
Hollins, S (1999) *Developmental Psychiatry: Insights from Learning Disability* Paper originally presented as the 1999 Blake Marsh Lecture at the Annual Meeting of The Royal College of Psychiatrists, Birmingham 29th June 1999
Hollins, S. and Evered, C. (1990) Group process and content: the challenge of mental handicap *Group Analysis* 23: 55-67
Hollins, S. & Esterhuyzen, A. (1997) Bereavement and grief in adults with learning disabilities *British Journal of Psychiatry* 170: 497-501
Hollins, S. & Grimer, M. (1988) *Pastoral Care and People with Mental Handicap* London: SPCK
Hollins, S. & Sinason, V. (2000) Psychotherapy, learning disabilities and trauma: new perspectives *British Journal of Psychiatry* 176: 32-36
Holmes, J. (2000) NHS Psychotherapy-past, future and present *British Journal of Psychotherapy* 16(4): 447-457
Howarth, J., Rodgers, J., Collins, A., Cook, B., Hamblett, G., Harris, C., Long, J., May, Z., & Webster, W. (2001) Difference and choice in *Considered Choices? The New Genetics, Prenatal Testing and People with Learning Disabilities*. Ward, L. (Ed.) Kidderminster, UK: BILD Publications

Institute of Medicine (1984). Bereavement during childhood and adolescence in *Bereavement: Reactions, Consequences and Care* pp.99-141 Washington, DC: National Academy Press

Jancar, J. (1990) Cancer and mental handicap: a further study *British Journal of Psychiatry* 156: 531-533

Judd, D. (1989) *Give Sorrow Words: Working With a Dying Child* London: Free Association Books

Jung, C.G. (1968) *The Archetypes and the Collective Unconscious* Princeton: Princeton University Press

Kahr, B. (1996) *Breaches of confidentiality in the history of psychoanalysis* (unpublished paper)

Kahr, B. (2000) Towards the creation of disability psychotherapists *The Psychotherapy Review* 2(9):420-23

Kane, B. (1979) Children's concept of death *Journal of Genetic Psychology* 134:141-153

Kempton, W. (1972) *Guidelines for Planning a Training Course on Human Sexuality and the Retarded* Philadelphia: Planned Parenthood Association of Southern Pennsylvania

Kitching, N. (1987) Helping people with mental handicaps cope with bereavement: a case study with discussion *Mental Handicap* (15): 60-63

Klass, D., Silverman, P. R. & Nickman, S. L. (1996) *Continuing Bonds, New Understandings of Grief* Philadelphia, USA: Taylor and Francis

Klein, M. (1940) Mourning and its relationship to manic depressive states *International Journal of Psycho-Analysis* 21: 125-53

Kloeppel, D. A. & Hollins, S. (1989) Double handicap: mental retardation and death in the family *Death Studies* 13: 31-38

Kohon, G. (1986) *The British School of Psychoanalysis: The Independent Tradition* London: Free Association

Kubler-Ross, E. (1969) *On Death and Dying* New York: Macmillan

Lahad, M. (1992) Story-making in assessment: method for coping with stress, in *Dramatherapy: Theory and Practice* (2) Jennings, S. (Ed.) London: Routledge

Landesman-Dwyer, S. & Berkson, G. (1984) Friendships and social behaviour in J. Wortis (Ed.) *Mental Retardation and Developmental Disabilities* 13, London: Plenum Press

Lewis, C.S. (1961) *A Grief Observed* New York: Bantam Books

Lifton, R. J. (1986) *The Nazi Doctors: Medical Killing and the Psychology of Genocide* London: Papermac

Lindemann, E. (1944) Symptomology and management of acute grief *American Journal of Psychiatry* 101: 141-8

Lipe-Goodson, P. S. & Goebel, B. L. (1983) Perceptions of age and death in mentally retarded adults *Mental Retardation* 21(2):68-75

Loach, E. (2003) *The Hardest Thing* UK: The Guardian Newspaper, Weekend Supplement, May 31st, 35-7

Lorenz, K. (1966) *On Aggression* New York: Harcourt Brace Jovanovich

Machin, L. (2003) Paper presented at roc Loss and Bereavement Conference May 2003 Herts, UK

Magrill, D. , Handley, P., Gleeson, S., Charles, D. and the Sharing Caring Project Steering Group (1997) *Crisis Approaching: The Situation Facing Sheffield's Elderly Carers of People with Learning Disabilities* Sheffield: Sharing Caring Project

Mahler, M., Pine, F& Bergman, A. (1975) *The Psychological Birth of the Human Infant* New York: Basic

Marks, D. (1999) *Disability: Controversial Debates and Psychosocial Perspectives* London: Routledge

Marris, P. (1958) *Widows and their Families* London: Routledge & Kegan Paul

Marris, P. (1974) *Loss and Change* London: Routledge & Kegan Paul

Marris, P. (1986) *Loss and Change*, 2nd edition London: Routledge

Marris, P. (1992) Grief, loss of meaning and society *Bereavement Care* 11(2):18-23

Marwit, S. J. & Klass, D. (1995) Grief and the role of the inner representation of the deceased. *Omega: Journal of Death And Dying* 30: 283-98

Mason, M. (1992) Internalised opression, in Rierser, R. & Mason, M. (Eds), *Disability Equality in the Classroom: A Human Rights Issue* London: Disability Equality in Education

Mattison, V. and Pistrang, N. (2000) *Saying Goodbye; When Keyworker Relationships End.* London: Free Association Books

McCarthy, M. (1999) *Sexuality and Women with Learning Disabilities.* London UK: Jessica Kingsley Pubs

McDermot, J.J. (1986) *Streams of Experience: Reflections in the History and Philosophy of American Culture* Amherst: University of Massachusetts Press

McEnhill, L. S. (1999) Guided mourning interventions, in *Living with Loss: Helping People with Learning Disabilities Cope with Bereavement and Loss* Blackman, N. (Ed.) Brighton UK: Pavilion Publishing

McAvoy, B. R. (1986) Death after Bereavement *British Medical Journal* 293:835-836

McLoughlin, I. J. (1986) Care of the dying: bereavement in the mentally handicapped. *British Journal of Hospital Medicine* 36: 256-260

Mencap Report (1998) *The NHS: Health for all? People with Learning Disabilities and Health Care* London, UK: Mencap National Centre

Mickelson, P. (1949) Can mentally deficient parents be helped to give their children better care?, *American Journal of Mental Deficiency* 53 (3): 516-34

Murphy, L. & Razza, N. (1998) Domestic violence against women with mental retardation in *Battered Women and their Families*, Roberts, A. (Ed,) (2nd Edn. pp. 271- 290) New York: Springer

Nagy, M. (1948) The child's theories concerning death *Journal of Genetic Psychology*, 73: 3-27

Nagy, M. (1959) The child's view of death in *The Meaning of Death* Feifel, H. (Ed.) (pp.79-98) New York: McGraw-Hill

Nirje, B. (1980) The normalisation principle in *Normalisation, Social Integration and Community Services* Flynn, R. & Nitsch, K. (Eds) Austin, Texas: Pro-Ed

O'Driscoll (2000) *Do the feebleminded have an emotional life? A history of psychotherapy and people with learning disabilities* (unpublished)

Oswin, M. (1971) *The Empty Hours: A Study of the Weekend Life of Handicapped Children in Institutions.* UK: The Penguin Press

Oswin, M. (1978) *Holes in the Welfare Net* London: Bedford Square Press.

Oswin, M. (1982) Nobody for me to look after *Parents' Voice* (March) p.10

Oswin, M. (1984) *They Keep Going Away – A Critical Study of Short-Term Residential Care Services for Children with Learning Difficulties* London, UK: King's Fund

Oswin, M. (1985) Bereavement in *Mental Handicap: A Multidisciplinary Approach,* M. Kraft M., Bicknell J., & Hollins, S. (Eds.), pp. 197-205. England: Bailliere Tindall

Oswin, M. (1989) Bereavement and Mentally Handicapped People. in *Last Things: Social work with the dying and bereaved* T. Philpot (Ed.) (pp. 92-105), Wellington, Surrey, Great Britain: Community Care

Oswin, M. (1991) *Am I Allowed to Cry? – A Study of Bereavement among People who have Learning Disabilities* London UK: Souvenir

Pantlin, A.W. (1985) Group analytic psychotherapy with mentally handicapped patients. *Group Analysis* 18: 44-50

Parkes, C. M. (1965) Bereavement and mental illness *British Journal of Medical Psychology* 38:1-12

Parkes, C. M. (1971) Psychosocial transitions: a field for study *Social Science and Medicine* 5(2) 101-14

Parkes, C. M. (1972) *Bereavement - Studies of Grief in Adult Life* London UK: Tavistock Publications

Parkes, C. M. (1975) *Bereavement* Harmondsworth, UK: Penguin

Parkes, C. M. (1988) Bereavement as a psychosocial transition: process of adaption to change *Journal of Social Issues* 44(3): 53-65

Parkes, C.M. (2003) *Attachment Patterns in Childhood: Relationships, Coping and Psychological States in Adults seeking Psychiatric Help after Bereavement* (in press) Paper delivered at the AGM of West Hertfordshire Bereavement Network

Parkes, C. M., Relf, M. & Couldrick, A. (1996) *Counselling in Terminal Care and Bereavement* Leicester: British Psychological Society

Parkes, C. M. & Weiss, R. S. (1983) *Recovery from Bereavement* Basic Books: New York

Payne, S. Horn, S & Relf, M. (1999) *Loss and Bereavement* Buckingham, UK: Open University Press

Persaud, S. & Persaud, M. (1997) Does it hurt to die? A description of bereavement work to help a group of people with learning disabilities who have suffered multiple, major losses. *Journal of Learning Disabilities for Nursing, Health and Social Care* 1(4):171-175

Pettingell, J. and Hart, S. (2001) Enhancing self-esteem through friendship? the possibilities for people with a learning disability *Mental Health Care* 4(10): 340-343

Piaget, J. (1954) *The Construction of Reality in the Child* (M. Cook, Trans) New York: Basic Books

Picton,S. (2001) What it means for us? in *Considered Choices? The New Genetics, Prenatal Testing and People with Learning Disabilities.* Ward, L. (Ed.) Kidderminster, UK: BILD Publications

Pierce Clark, L. (1933) *The Nature and Treatment of Amentia* London: Balliere

Prior, L. (1989) *The Social Organization of Death* London: Macmillan

Proctor, R. (1988) *Racial Hygeine: Medicine and the Nazis* Cambridge: Harvard University Press

Raphael, B. (1984) *The Anatomy of Bereavement* London: Hutchinson

Ray, R. (1977) The mentally handicapped child's reaction to bereavement. *Health Visitor* 51: 333-334

Raynor, E. (1991) *The Independent Mind in British Psychoanalysis* London: Free Association Books

Read, S. (1996) Helping people with learning disabilities to grieve. *British Journal of Nursing* 5(2): 91-95

Read, S. (1999) Creative ways of working when exploring the bereavement counselling process in *Living with Loss: Helping People with Learning Disabilities Cope with Bereavement and Loss* Blackman, N. (Ed.) Brighton UK: Pavilion Publishing

Read, S., Frost, I., Messenger, N. & Oates, S. (1999) Bereavement counselling and support for people with a learning disabilitiy: identifying issues and exploring possibilities *British Journal of Learning Disabilities*, 27: 99-104

Rendall, D. (1997) Fatherhood and learning disabilities: a personal account of reaction and resolution *Journal of Learning Disabilities for Nursing, Health and Social Care* 1(2): 77-83

Rindnitzki, G. (1988) Group therapy with disturbed young people: effects of modified group-analytic techniques *Group Analysis* 21:169-180

Rix, B. (1990) *The History of Mental Handicap and the Development of Mencap* 14th Annual Stanley Segal Lecture, University of Nottingham

Robertson, J. (1953) Some responses of young children to the loss of maternal care *Nursing Times* 49: 382-3866

Robertson, J., Emerson, E., Gregory, N., Hatton, C., Kessissoglou, S., Hallam, A. & Linehan, C. (2001) Social networks of people with intellectual disabilities in residential settings *Mental Retardation* 39:201-24

Royal College of Psychiatrists' Working Group (2002) *Psychotherapy and Learning Disability* McGinnity, Dr M. (Chairperson) & Banks, Dr R. (Secretary). Poster presented at IASSID European congress. Dublin

Rubin, S. S. (1996) The wounded family: bereaved parents and the impact of adult child loss in *Continuing Bonds: New Understandings of Grief* Klass, D., Silverman, P. R. and Nickman, S. L. (Eds.) Philadelphia, US: Taylor and Francis

Scally, B. (1973) Marriage and mental handicap: some observations in Northern Ireland in *Human Sexuality and the Mentally Retarded* de la Cruz, F. & LaVeck, G. (Eds) New York, NY: Brunner/Mazel

Schaffer, H, R. (1958) Objective observations of personality development in early infancy *British Journal of Medical Psychology* 31: 174-183

Shackleton, C. H. (1984) *Advanced Behavioral Research* 6: 153-205

Shakespeare, T. (2000) Foreword, in *Considered Choices? The new genetics, prenatal testing and people with learning disabilities* Ward, L. (Ed.) Kidderminster, UK: BILD Publications

Shorr, M. & Speed, M. N. (1963) Delinquency as a manifestation of the mourning process. *Psychiatric Quarterly* 37:540-558

Shuchter, S.R. & Zisook, S. (1993) The course of normal grief, in *Handbook of Bereavement*, Stroebe, M.S., Stroebe, W. & Hansson, R.O. (Eds.) Cambridge: Cambridge University Press

Silverman, P.R. (1986) *Widow to Widow* New York: Springer Publishing Company

Simpson, D. (2002) Learning disability as a refuge from knowledge *Psychoanalytic Psychotherapy* 16(3): 215-226

Sinason, V. (1986) Secondary mental handicap and its relationship to trauma, *Psychoanalytic Psychotherapy* 2(2): 131-54

Sinason, V. (1992) *Mental Handicap and the Human Condition* Free Association Books

Smilansky, S. (1987) *On Death: Helping Children Understand and Cope.* New York: Peter Lang

Smith, H. & Brown, H. (1989) Whose community, whose care? in *Making Connections: Reflecting on the Lives and Experiences of People with Learning Difficulties* Brechin, A. & Walmsey, J. (Eds.) pp. 229-36 London: Hodder and Stoughton

Sovner, R. & Hurley, A.D. (1983) Do the mentally retarded suffer from affective illness? *Archive of General Psychiatry* 40:61-67

Spitz, R. (1957) *No and Yes* New York: International Universities Press

Strachan, J. G. (1981) Reactions to bereavement; a study of a group of hospital residents *Mental Handicap* 9(1) 20-21

Stokes, J. and Sinason, V. (1992) Secondary mental handicap as a defence in *Psychotherapy and Mental Handicap* Waitman, A. and Conboy-Hill, S. (Eds.) London: Sage

Strickler, H. L. (2001) Interaction between family violence and mental retardation. *Mental Retardation* 39(6): 461-471

Stroebe, M. S. and Stroebe, W. (1987) *Bereavement and Health* Cambridge: Cambridge University Press

Stroebe, M.S., Stroebe, W. & Hansson, R.O. (Eds). (1993) *Handbook of Bereavement* Cambridge: Cambridge University Press

Stroebe, M.S. & Schut, H. (1999) The dual process model of coping with bereavement: rationale and description. *Death Studies* 23: 197-224

Symington, N. (1981) The psychotherapy of a subnormal patient *The British Journal of Medical Psychology* 54: 187-199

Symington, N. (1986) *The Analytic Experience: Lectures from the Tavistock* London: Free Association Books

Thomas, K. R. (1997) Countertransference and disability: some observations. *Journal of Melanie Klein and Object Relations* 15(1) 145-161

Thompson, D. (2002) in Foundation for People with Learning Disabilities Report: *Today and Tomorrow: The Report of the Growing Older with Learning Disabilities Programme* London: Mental Health Foundation

Todd, S. (2002) Death does not become us: the absence of death and dying in Intellectual disability research *Journal of Gerontological Social Work* 38 (No.s1&2): 225-239

Tomm, K. (1990) In Foreword to White, M. & Epston, D., *Narrative Means to Therapeutic Ends* New York USA: W.W. Norton & Co

Tuffrey-Wigne, (2003) I. The palliative care needs of people with intellectual disabilities: a literature review *Palliative Medicine* 17: 55-62

Tyson-Rawson, K. (1996) Relationship and heritage: manifestations of ongoing attachment following father death in *Continuing Bonds, New Understandings of Grief* Klass, D., Silverman, P. S. & Nickman, S. L (Eds). Philadelphia, USA: Taylor and Francis

UK Health Department Report (2000) *Secondary Healthcare for People with a Learning Disability* London: Department of Health

UK Department Of Health (2001a) *Valuing People: A New Strategy for Learning Disability for the 21st Century* London: Department of Health

UK Department of Health (2001b) *Family Matters: Counting Families* London: Department of Health

Valentine, D. P. (1990) Double jeopardy: child maltreatment and mental retardation. *Child and Adult Social Work* 7: 487-499

Von Franz, M.L. (1987) *Interpretation of Fairytales* Dallas, Texas, US: Spring Publications

Walker, C., Ryan, T. & Walker, A. (1996) *Fair Shares for All: Disparities in Service Provision for Different Groups of People with Learning Difficulties Living in the Community* Brighton: Pavilion Publishing, & York: Joseph Rowntree Foundation

Walker, C. & Walker, A. (1998) *Uncertain Futures: People with Learning Difficulties and their Ageing Family Carers* Brighton: Pavilion Publishing, & York: Joseph Rowntree Foundation

Wallace, W. (2000) *National/London Learning Disability Strategy* Paper presented at the Conference of the Psychologists' Special Interest group in Learning Disabilities, Abergavenny, Wales

Walter, T. 1996 A new model of grief: bereavement and biography *Mortality* 1(1) 7-25

Ward, C. (1998) *Preparing for a Positive Future: Meeting the Age Related Needs of Older People with Learning Disabilities* Chesterfield: ARC

Ward, L. (2001) *Considered Choices? The New Genetics, Prenatal Testing and People with Learning Disabilities* Kidderminster, UK: BILD Publications

Watson, L. & Harker, M. (1993) *Community Care Planning: A Model for Housing Need Assessment* London: Institute of Housing and National Federation of Housing Associations

Winnicott, D.W. (1954) A primary state of being: pre-primitive stages, in *Human Nature* London: Free Association Books, 1988

Wolfensberger, W. (1972) *The Principle of Normalisation in Human Services* Toronto: National Institute on Mental Retardation

Wolfensberger, W. (1983) Social role valorization: A proposed new term for the principle of normalisation *Mental Retardation* 21: 234-239

Wolfenstein, M. (1966) How is mourning possible? *Psychoanalytic study of the child* 21: 93-123

Wolff, S. (1969) *Children Under Stress: Understanding the Emotionally Disturbed Child* Harmondsworth, UK: Penguin Books

Worden, J. W. (1983) *Grief Counselling and Grief Therapy* New York: Springer Publishing

Worden, J. W. (1991) (2nd Edn.) *Grief Counselling and Grief Therapy: A handbook for the mental health practitioner* London, UK: Routledge

Worden, J.W. (1996) *Children and Grief: When a Parent Dies* New York: Guilford Press

Wortman, C. B. & Silver, R. C. (1989) The myth of coping with loss *Journal of Clinical Consulting Psychology* 57:349-357

Yanok, J. & Beifus, J, A. (1993) Communication about loss and mourning: death education for individuals with mental retardation. *Mental Retardation* 31(3) 144-147

Zisook, S. & DeVaul, R.A. (1976) Grief related facsimile illness *International Journal of Psychiatric Medicine* 7:329-336

Resources

USEFUL ARTICLES AND BOOKS

Atkinson, D., Jackson, M. & Walmsey, J. (1997) *Forgotten Lives: Exploring the History of Learning Disability* Kidderminster, UK:BILD

• Accounts of lives in the long stay learning disability institutions of the twentieth century.

Blackman, N. (Ed.) (1999) *Living with Loss: Helping People with Learning Disabilities Cope with Bereavement and Loss* Brighton, UK: Pavilion Publishing

• A series of chapters describing pioneering work and experiences in the field of loss and people with learning disabilities

Day, P. and Smith, J. (1996) Learning about life's changes and working through loss *Practice* 8:1

• A useful paper which describes the setting up and operation of a group in a day centre. Aimed to help people with learning disabilities understand gains and losses at different life stages

Hodges, S. (2003) *Counselling Adults with Learning Disabilities* Hampshire, UK: Palgrave

• A comprehensive guide for counsellors considering working with people with learning disabilities

Luchterhand, C. & Murphy, N. (1988) *Helping Adults with Mental Retardation Grieve a Death Loss* Philadelphia, USA: Accelerated Development

Moss, S. C. (1993) *The Mini PAS-ADD (Psychiatric Assessment Schedules for Adults with a Developmental Disability)* The Hester Adrian Research Centre University of Manchester

Nottingham Healthcare NHS Trust Learning Disability Directorate (1999) - Bereavement Guidelines

• An excellent guide for residential services. It offers recommendations for good practice in the management of bereavement experienced by residents

Persaud, S. & Persaud, M. (1997) Does it hurt to die? A description of bereavement work to help a group of people with learning disabilities who have suffered multiple, major losses *Journal of Learning Disabilities for Nursing, Health and Social Care* 1(4):171-175

• A paper describing a death education group for people with learning disabilities

BOOKS AND PACKS TO USE AS TOOLS

Cathcart, F. (1994) *Understanding Death and Dying* (Series). Worcestershire: British Institute of Learning Disabilities.

• A series of three books each explaining death and dying in a straightforward way. Targeted at three different groups: people with learning disabilities, staff and professionals, and a third for families.

Cooley, J. & McGauran, F. *Talking Together About Death - A bereavement pack for people with learning disabilities, their families and carers* Bicester, UK: Speechmark Publishing

• A pack of five sets of black-and-white illustrated cards, depicting the life-cycle and various aspects of death and mourning, such as a graveside scene, a coffin etc. Includes a user's guide.

Heegaard, M. (1988) *When Someone Very Special Dies* USA: Woodland Press

• A workbook designed for children, which encourages drawing and simple written pieces about feelings

Holland, A., Payne, A. and Vickery, L (1998) *Exploring Your Emotions* Worcestershire, UK: British Institute of Learning Disabilities. • A set of 30 colour photographs illustrating common emotions that can be used as a tool to help people talk about and reflect upon feelings. A manual is included.

Hollins, S. & Sireling, L (1991) *Understanding Grief: Working with Grief and People who have Learning Disabilities* Brighton, UK: Pavilion Publishing

• Training pack which can be used in formal formal staff training or as an educational tool for families and carers of a bereaved person with learning disabilities. The pack includes a video and a copy of *When Dad Died* (a *Book Beyond Words*, see below)

Books Beyond Words

• There are several useful books in the *Books Beyond Words* Series (Gaskell/St. George's Hospital Medical School, London SW17). This series of books tell stories on important and often difficult life themes, including death and bereavement, in pictures. Some of these are listed below:

Hollins, S & Sireling, L. (1989) *When Dad Died* London: St. George's Hospital Medical School

Hollins, S & Sireling, L. (1989) *When Mum Died* London: St. George's Hospital Medical School

Hollins, S., Dowling, S. & Blackman, N. (2003) *When Somebody Dies* London: St. George's Hospital Medical School

Luchterhand, C. & Murphy, N. (1998) *Helping Adults with Mental Retardation Grieve a Death Loss* Accelerated Development (USA): Taylor and Francis (UK)

• This book lists plenty of ideas for supporting people with learning disabilities as they cope with bereavement.

Persaud, S. & Persaud, M. (2003) *Loss and Bereavement For People with Learning Disabilities*. Derbyshire NHS Mental Health Services NHS Trust. Wordsmith Publications. Buckinghamshire. UK.

• A bereavement information pack which aims to provide carers of people with learning disabilities with some practical indicators enabling them to support people who have experienced loss or bereavement. It contains pictures, signs and symbols to be used as a resource.

Slater, D. & De Wit, M. (1999) *Rediscovering Our Selves: The Recovery and Communication of the Lived Experience of People with Learning Disabilities*. Brighton, UK: Pavilion Publishing

• A training pack and video that promotes creative ideas for reminiscence with people with learning disabilities.

Stuart, M. (1997) *Looking Back, Looking Forward: Reminiscence with People with Learning Difficulties* Brighton, UK: Pavilion Publishing

• A training pack which encourages the use of reminiscence with people with learning disabilities

VIDEOS

Speak Up Self Advocacy. (1997) *Coping with Death*. Speak Up Self Advocacy, 43 Holm Flatt Street, Parkgate, Rotherham, South Yorkshire, S62 6HJ. Tel 01709 710199

• A video made by and for people with learning disabilities. It explains what happens when somebody dies.

SERVICES

Cruse Bereavement Care is the national organisation for bereaved people. Many counsellors are now offering their services to people with learning disabilities. *Contact:* Cruse Bereavement Care, Cruse House, 126 Sheen Road, Surrey TW9 1UR. Tel: 020 8939 9530. *Day by Day* is the Cruse National Helpline 0870 167 1677. Helpline @ crusebereavementcare.co.uk

• Provides support and information about local bereavement counselling services. It is worth contacting local bereavement services to find out whether they offer counselling to people with learning disabilities. If they do not, this could be because they have not thought of it before. With the right support, they may consider it (see Chapter10).

Respond helpline 0800808 0700

• Supports people with learning disabilities, their carers and professionals around any issue of trauma, including bereavement.

Most community learning disability teams should be able offer some bereavement counselling from their psychology services, Arts therapies practitioners and/or counsellors or psychotherapists who make up their team.

The roc Loss and Bereavement Service offers a therapy service to people with learning disabilities, and training and support to carers throughout Hertfordshire. It is a unique service provided by the Hertfordshire Partnership NHS Trust and there is therefore no charge to users of the service. However, they also provide training to generic counsellors and therapists from any region.

They can be contacted at the following address: roc, Hertfordshire Partnership Trust, Woodside Road, Abbots Langley, Herts, WD5 0HT, Tel. 01923 663628